The 12 Essentials
for
Disciple-Making

5032 Palm Ave
95841

The 12 Essentials for Disciple-Making

(Everyone's Ministry)

Dr. Joseph Arthur

To order additional copies of this book, contact:
Xlibris Corporation
1-888-795-4274
www.Xlibris.com
Orders@Xlibris.com
60298

Contents

This book is dedicated to

all those who are Christian disciple-makers

"It is good to have an end to journey towards;
but it is the journey that matters in the end"

Ursula K. LeGuin

ACKNOWLEDGMENTS

This book has been a team effort and would not be possible without the gracious experiences of a host of church and office staff.

Special thanks to Owen Stricklin who was convinced that Disciple-Making is the Biblical way, and necessary for Kingdom Growth. He went out of his way to encourage me to have the thoughts in this book published. Barbara Stricklin took the risk of implementing the strategy of disciple-making at The First United Methodist Church in Deland, Florida.

A hard working team consisting of Ann Brandon, Lynn Bear, and Cathy Arthur, brought together the many details needed to complete this book. I am especially fond of the three of them and particularly the latter.

If imitation is the highest form of compliment, then I owe thanks to many that I have borrowed from in terms of ideas and spirit.

De Vern Fromke, ***Unto Full Stature,*** gave me full confidence in presenting the Gospel and its daily implications.

Carl F. George, ***The Coming Church Revolution,*** conducted substantial study and organized his findings to challenge me.

Steven Collins, in ***Christian Discipleship,*** a disciple-maker himself inspired me to become a disciple-maker.

Tom Stebbins, ***Friendship Evangelism by the Book,*** taught me the importance of applying first century principles to twenty-first century relationships.

James Belasco and Ralph Stayer, ***Flight of the Buffalo,*** gave me the challenge to see the potential to change the church by seeing how it perceives leadership in the church.

Gene A. Getz, ***The Walk,*** expanded the concept of how our personal journey has meaningful relationships and fulfillment when we go back and implement the basics.

Richard J. Foster, ***Celebration of Discipline,*** was a great help in understanding the path to spiritual growth.

Rick Rusaw and Eric Swanson, **The Externally Focused Chuch,** emphasized our church is not growing spiritually if its members are not serving.

We trust this book, through the Holy Spirit, will lift your hearts, awaken a determination to press toward the cross, and inspire you to God's perfect will, as you seek first, not the plans of noble men, but the glorious Kingdom of God.

INTRODUCTION

GOD WANTS TO USE YOU!

It is hoped that this study on disciple-making will motivate you to become all that God intends for you to become. God honors faithfulness based on the way we carry out His instructions. This is a call back to the basics of fulfilling the Great Commission. Jesus said:

> **God authorized and commanded me to commission you: Go out and train everyone you meet, far and near, in this way of life, marking them by baptism in the threefold name: Father, Son, and Holy Spirit. Then instruct them in the practice of all I have commanded you. I'll be with you as you do this, day after day after day, right up to the end of the age.**

> **(Matthew 28:18-20)**

The purpose of this Manual is to help individuals and churches to experience "Christ is in you, so therefore you can look forward to sharing in God's glory." (Colossians 1:27)

We are to dedicate ourselves to leading people to Christ and establishing these new believers in the Christian faith until they themselves become disciple-makers.

CHAPTER ONE

CROSSING OVER:
Developing a Personal Relationship with God

The divine way of life God intends for man is not an intellectual knowledge, but an opening of the spiritual eyes of the heart of man.

> **I ask—ask the God of our Master, Jesus Christ, the God of glory—to make you intelligent and discerning in knowing him personally, your eyes focused and clear, so that you can see exactly what it is he is calling you to do, grasp the immensity of this glorious way of life he has for his followers, oh, the utter extravagance of his work in us who trust him—endless energy, boundless strength!**

> **(Ephesians 1:17-19)**

God, the creator of the universe, loves all people.

When God created the first human beings, Adam and Eve, He placed them in the Garden of Eden and He walked and talked with them. He loved His creation and enjoyed having a personal relationship with them. He loved them and wanted them to love Him. He didn't want them to be like robots, so He created them with a human will so they could make choices. He loved His creation so much He provided everything they needed. They could partake of everything He had provided with one exception: "Do not eat of the tree of knowledge of good and evil." If they obeyed Him He would know how much they really loved Him.

So, what actually happened? Satan, the enemy of God, convinced Adam and Eve to turn inward to a life of getting for themselves instead of a life of giving themselves back to God in obedience. This selfishness is what God calls **sin**. We all live selfish lives. It is sin that destroys our relationship with God.

> **It is obvious what kind of life develops out of trying to get your own way all the time: repetitive, loveless, cheap sex; a stinking accumulation of mental and emotional garbage; frenzied and joyless grabs for happiness; trinket gods; magic-show religion; paranoid loneliness; cutthroat competition; all-consuming-yet-never-satisfied wants; a brutal temper; an impotence to love or be loved; divided homes and divided lives; small-minded and lopsided pursuits; the vicious habit of depersonalizing everyone into a rival; uncontrolled and uncontrollable addictions; ugly parodies of community. I could go on.**

> **(Galatians 5:19-21)**

The message of the Bible is for the entire human race. All human beings need affirmation and forgiveness. We all have committed sins that people know about and sins that nobody knows. Many of our sins are known only to us and to God.

> **Basically, all of us, whether insiders or outsiders, start out in identical conditions, which is to say that we all start out as sinners. Scripture leaves no doubt about it: There's nobody living right, not even one, nobody who knows the score, nobody alert for God. They've all taken the wrong turn; they've all wandered down blind alleys. No one's living right; I can't find a single one . . . .**

> **This makes it clear, doesn't it, that whatever is written in these Scriptures is not what God says *about others* but *to us* to whom these Scriptures were addressed in the first place! And**

it's clear enough, isn't it, that we're sinners, every one of us, in the same sinking boat with everybody else?"

(Romans 3:10-12)

God wants us to repent of our sin.

When we confess to God that we are sinners, turn from our sinful ways, and go in the opposite direction, this process is called **repentance**. Many people believe they can save themselves by doing good works. Good deeds are important but they do not provide what God demands. Since we cannot save ourselves, we must not deceive ourselves by thinking we can distract God from seeing our sins. We need God's forgiveness because we are conceived and born in sin; we sin daily; and we cannot enter heaven without God's forgiveness.

You didn't think, did you, that just by pointing your finger at others you would distract God from seeing all your misdoings and from coming down on you hard? Or did you think that because he's such a nice God, he'd let you off the hook? Better think this one through from the beginning. God is kind, but he's not soft. In kindness he takes us firmly by the hand and leads us into a radical life-change.

(Romans 2:3-4)

When we are confronted with our sin, the question is "What will I do about it?" You have several options. These options may be:

Helpful, harmful, or just hot air

. . . You can try to be righteous on your own, but it never works.

. . . You can ignore it, but your sin still remains.

. . . You can try to do better, but it does not last.

. . . You can give way to despair and it ends in defeat.

. . . You can use the lemon approach and become sour toward life.

. . . You can endeavor to drown your sorrow in drink and drugs and reveal your stupidity.

. . . You can live a life of waywardness and wickedness and end imprisoned.

. . . You can put your faith in Jesus Christ and turn your life over to God and find meaning in life.

These are the choices open to you. Turning your life over to God makes the most sense. "There is no conversion without a crisis; there is no birth without painful travail; there is no salvation without agonizing repentance."[1] We must face who we really are, and know that there is no new life without repentance. If you feel abandoned by God, remember God still loves all human beings. Repenting of your sin is an opportunity to be cleansed and set free. By confessing our sins before God, we also confess our reliance upon God's grace and mercy. The measure of mercy received depends on our willingness to admit our shortcomings. We do not deserve God's forgiveness; forgiveness is grace.

God wants to have a relationship with us.

In spite of our sin, whenever we repent, God is merciful because He loves us and grants us forgiveness. We need forgiveness so we can have a personal relationship with God. This forgiveness is provided for all who receive Jesus Christ, Who is God's unique Son. God the Father could do this because Jesus Christ came to earth and lived a perfect life before us. While He was on earth, He died on the cross to pay the penalty for our sin. Because our heavenly Father loves us so much, He placed all our sins on His Son, Jesus Christ. Jesus rose from the dead to purchase us a place in heaven. It is a gift and received by faith.

All people have some kind of faith. They believe in something or in someone. They may even believe that Jesus Christ existed. Saving faith, however, is trusting Jesus Christ alone for our Salvation. Jesus Christ, being very God, has no beginning and no ending. He is eternal life, and He comes by His Holy Spirit to live in all those who put their faith in Him as their Savior and Lord.

> **There once was a man, his name John, sent by God to point out the way to the Life-Light. He came to show everyone where to look, who to believe in. John was not himself the Light; he was there to show the way to the Light. The Life-Light was**

the real thing: every person entering Life he brings into Light. He was in the world, the world was there through him, and yet the world didn't even notice. He came to his own people, but they didn't want him. But whoever did want him, who believed he was who he claimed and would do what he said, he made to be their true selves, their child-of-God selves.

(John 1:6-12)

Forgiveness is where we encounter God's goodness and mercy. Our battles are within ourselves. We struggle with psychological guilt feelings, guilt, shame, and remorse. We all have done things we wish we had never done. How often have we wounded others with our words that we would like to take back. We have held hatred, jealousies, and prejudices. Yes, people everywhere are the same. We need forgiveness, faith, hope, and love.

God offers us the gifts of grace and forgiveness through His Son Jesus Christ. We long for the gift of grace. Yet we feel we don't deserve it. That is why God's forgiveness is grace. It is true we don't deserve it. Forgiveness is more than a gift; it is life.

I am reminded of Jesus' words:

I am the Road, also the Truth, also the Life. No one gets to the Father apart from me.

(John 14:6)

Jesus was either the world's biggest and worst liar, or He is the Way, the Truth, and the Life. Jesus asked Peter, "Who do you say that I am?" Peter said, "You are Christ, the Son of the living God." We all have to come to terms with the historical person called Jesus Christ. You either accept Him or reject Him.

God wants us to cross over the bridge from our side to His side.

We are on a journey we call life. God the creator wants to have a personal relationship with us. We have sinned and have a broken relationship with God. But God has made a bridge so that we can walk over it and have our relationship with God restored. That bridge is called the cross. Jesus paid the penalty for our sin. God now looks at us as if we had never sinned. What does it mean to cross over? It has a present and future meaning:

The **present** meaning is to receive the Lord Jesus Christ as our Savior by grace through faith.

> **Now God has us where he wants us, with all the time in this world and the next to shower grace and kindness upon us in Christ Jesus. Saving is all his idea, and all his work. All we do is trust him enough to let him do it. It's God's gift from start to finish! We don't play the major role. If we did, we'd probably go around bragging that we'd done the whole thing! No, we neither make nor save ourselves. God does both the making and saving. He creates each of us by Christ Jesus to join him in the work he does, the good work he has gotten ready for us to do, work we had better be doing.**
>
> **(Ephesians 2:7-10)**

God wants to have a relationship with us. He wants this relationship to be one of where God shows His love to people and where people show their love to Him. However, we have rebelled against him and broken off that relationship.[2]

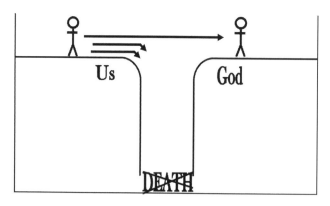

This rebellion is what we call "sin." Sin is disobeying God. When someone is offended it causes problems in the relationship. Sin causes a separation between God and man. Most of us are aware of this and try to do things to get back to God, but it doesn't work. Furthermore, the sins we have committed have to be punished, and that punishment is death. That is bad news.[3]

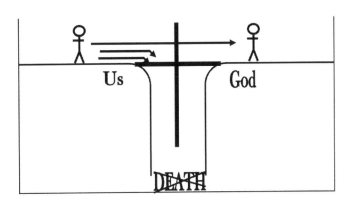

But God did for us what we could not do and that is build a bridge back to Himself. God took care of the sin problem by sending His Son, Jesus Christ, to live a perfect life, then die on the cross in order that a person's sin could be forgiven. The amazing thing is after Jesus was dead and buried, He rose from the dead, proving God has the power to save people from sin and death. This is the "Good News."

One last thing. It is not enough just to know this. We have to act on it by admitting that we have rebelled and that we want His forgiveness and leadership. It is only as you believe in Christ as your Lord and Savior that you cross over the separation caused by your sin and begin a personal relationship with God. This word "believe" is more than just believing that Jesus Christ exists. It means to trust Christ and Him alone to make you right with God.

May we personalize this for a moment? The question now is, how can a person cross over the bridge that Christ has provided? The Bible says whoever believes in Him will cross over to God and receive eternal life. Does this make sense to you? Where would you place yourself on this diagram? Is there any reason why you would not want to cross over to the other side?

You can lead a horse to water but you can't make him drink

Cicero lived before Christ was born but he made the observation that you can't confer a benefit on an unwilling object. Now, if you are willing and really want the gift of eternal life, you can pray to God right now. If you want to cross over the bridge and begin experiencing the abundant life, you can call on Him and ask Him for this gift right now. Here is a suggested prayer you might want to use:

"Lord Jesus, I know that I am a sinner and separated from you. Forgive me of my sin. I believe Jesus Christ died for my sins and rose from the dead to purchase for me a place in heaven. Come into my life and save me. I repent of my sin and place my trust in you for my salvation. I open the door of my heart and invite you into my life. Amen."

If that prayer is the desire of your heart, and you sincerely prayed that prayer, today is your spiritual birthday!

I _____   _____

(Fill in with your name)

prayed to invite Jesus Christ into my life as my Lord and Savior on this

_____

(Fill in with the date: month, day, year)

The **present** meaning to cross over the bridge is that you have personally prayed to trust in Jesus Christ as your Lord and Savior. The **future** meaning is a promise that we find in John's Gospel.

> **Don't let this throw you. You trust God, don't you? Trust me. There is plenty of room for you in my Father's home. If that weren't so, would I have told you that I'm on my way to get a room ready for you? And if I'm on my way to get your room ready, I'll come back and get you so you can live where I live.**
>
> **(John 14:1-3)**

God wants you to know you have the gift of Eternal Life.

John the apostle, knowing that the enemy of God will attempt to steal the confidence from new believers, writes:

> **This is the testimony in essence: God gave us eternal life; the life is in his Son. So, whoever has the Son, has life; who-ever**

rejects the Son, rejects life. My purpose in writing is simply this: that you who believe in God's Son will know beyond the shadow of a doubt that you have eternal life, the reality and not the illusion.

(I John 5:11-13)

The Bible gives us assurance that we have received the gift of eternal life. God also assures us that we are God's children by confirmation of the Holy Spirit.

God's Spirit touches our spirits and confirms who we really are. We know who he is, and we know who we are: Father and children.

(Romans 8:16)

Who wants to get hit by a truck?

Even though we have professed to have received Jesus Christ as our Savior, we may have doubts. Doubts can make us feel like we have been hit by a truck. Doubt may occur for several reasons:

1. We do not humble ourselves before God.
2. Pride can cause us to doubt God, The Bible, and God's Grace.
3. Sometimes individuals make childhood decisions, and later in life they question if they really became a Christian. Parents should explain the Gospel and encourage the children to pray and receive Jesus Christ as their Savior as soon as they are old enough to understand. Children who have made decisions early in life should reaffirm their faith in Christ when they reach the teenage years or at the time of confirmation.
4. A bitter spirit or resentment towards another allows doubt to creep into one's life. I was talking to an acquaintance who told me that a man murdered his brother. He said, "I could never forgive that man and so probably God will not forgive me." An unforgiving spirit can cause you to doubt salvation.
5. Selfish living is a major cause of doubt about whether or not we are a Christian.

My counsel is this: Live freely, animated and motivated by God's Spirit. Then you won't feed the compulsions of selfishness. For there is a root of sinful self-interest in us that is at odds with a free spirit, just as the free spirit is incompatible with selfishness.

(Galatians 5:16-17)

One day a young man on a farm experienced a flood of doubts about whether or not he really was a Christian. He walked outside behind the barn, knelt down, and prayed. His prayer contained the following:

"Thank you, God, for loving me and sending Your Son, the Lord Jesus Christ, to die for me, a sinner. Right now, I do receive Jesus Christ as my Savior. I ask you to cleanse me from all sin and make me Your child. Thank You for raising Jesus up from the dead as a living Savior, and thank You for hearing and answering this prayer."

He finished his prayer, pounded a wooden stake into the ground, and wrote the date on it. About two weeks later the doubts came back again. This time he had a ready and very effective reply. "All right, Satan, come with me!" He walked out behind the barn, pointed to the stake, and said, "See, Satan. here's the date and place I received Jesus Christ as my Savior. And God has promised that if I call upon the name of the Lord, I shall be saved." (Romans 10:13).

Those who sincerely repent of their sins and place their faith in Jesus Christ alone for their Salvation, will:

➢ begin to experience a new love for others.
➢ hunger to learn more about God's Word.
➢ develop a greater awareness of right and wrong.
➢ share with others about how God has brought about radical change in their lives.
➢ desire to be baptized as baptism is the beginning life on a new basis.

That's what baptism into the life of Jesus means. When we are lowered into the water, it is like the burial of Jesus; when we are raised up out of the water, it is like the resurrection of Jesus. Each of us is raised into a light-filled world by

our Father so that we can see where we're going in our new grace-sovereign country.

(Roman 6:4)

Understanding what's important from God's perspective is a challenge. If we could see earth from eternity, what we strive for during our years on earth would look different. Forgiveness! Faith! Hope! Love! These are far more important than material possessions. Here is a preview of the next chapter. We will see how God the Father's plan progresses from our being His **created** sons to becoming His **glorified** sons.

Application

1. God _created + loves_ all the human race.
2. What destroys our relationship with God? _Sin /Pride_
3. The message of the Bible is for _all_ the human race.
4. When we confess our sin and turn from it and go in the opposite direction, this process is called _repentence_.
5. We need _forgiveness_ because we are all sinful.
6. God wants to have a _Personal_ with us.
7. _Saving faith_ is trusting Jesus Christ alone for our salvation.
8. God offers us a _gift_ of grace.
9. The bridge from our side to His side is called _the Cross_.
10. What does it mean to "cross over"?

   a. _to recieve God_
   b. _promise of enternity recieve a place in heaven_

11. How do I know I have received the gift of Eternal Life?

   a. _bible tell me so_
   b. _holy spirit_

12. Name two things that will happen in your life when you become a Christian.
   hunger to learn more about God
   greater awarness of Right + Wrong

Assignment

1. Begin to pray about finding a person of the same sex to whom you could teach this lesson.
2. If you have never been baptized, contact your discipler to make arrangements with the pastor to be baptized.

CHAPTER TWO

FROM GLORY TO GLORY:
Unfolding The Father's Plan for Me

The eternal, self-sufficient, sovereign God stands above all else in His glory!

> **Is there anyone around who can explain God? Anyone smart enough to tell him what to do? Anyone who has done him such a huge favor that God has to ask his advice?**
>
> **Everything comes from him;**
> **Everything happens through him;**
> **Everything ends up in him."**

(Romans 11:35-36)

In the following eleven sessions we are going to focus on how Jesus lived and told us to live. You will be learning about eleven more ESSENTIALS of DISCIPLE-MAKING to help you become a successful disciple-maker.

The second essential of becoming a successful disciple-maker is to understand the Father's plan as it relates to me. God moves human beings along a progressive plan that takes us through four stages.

Let's begin to understand life's journey. There is no better place to start than at the beginning. "We tend to think of our journey of faith as linear. It has a starting point, salvation, and an ending point, heaven. Scripture would seem to indicate that a disciple's relationship with God is more dynamic."[4]

A circle may describe our life in a more dynamic way.

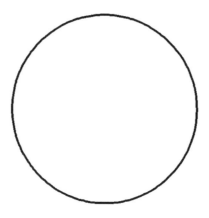

Stage 1: Created Sons of God

The first stage in the circle of life would be as created sons of God.

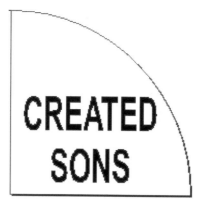

We do have a beginning, but after death life continues on. The Bible tells where we came from, why we are here, and where we will be going when we leave this earth. We each have a great opportunity to enter into a dynamic life.

As we discuss our journey of life we will use the term *man* to refer to the entire human race.

So God created man in his own image, in the image of God he created him; male and female he created them.

(Genesis 1:27 NIV)

From the very beginning man was created to bring glory to God.

It's in Christ that we find out who we are and what we are living for. Long before we first heard of Christ and got our hopes up, he had his eye on us, had designs on us for glorious living, part of the overall purpose he is working out in everything and everyone.

(Ephesians 1:11-12)

Scripture tells us that we were created to glorify God, indicating we are important to God. It is not wrong for God to seek glory for Himself because He is the creator of all things and, therefore, not taking glory away from anyone. It is wrong for man to seek glory for himself because he would be taking glory away from God. Only God deserves glory.

Out of all the creatures God made, only one creature, man, is said to be made "in the image of God." What does that mean? The word *image* refers to something similar but not identical. It means we are like God and represent God, but we are not God.

The **first** thing God created in relation to man was a **physical body**. We should not think that our physical bodies imply that God has a material body. But there are some ways in which our bodies reflect something of God's own character and constitute part of what it means to be created in the image of God. Our physical bodies give us the ability to see with our own eyes. This is a God-like characteristic because God sees. Our ears give us the ability to hear. God hears. Our mouths give us the ability to speak. God speaks. Our senses of taste, touch, and smell give us the ability to enjoy God's creation. Our physical bodies are the means by which man can experiment and communicate with his physical environment.

Without our physical bodies we would not be able to communicate with other human beings.

> **The Lord God formed the man from the dust of the ground and breathed into his nostrils the breath of life, and the man became a living being.**

> **(Genesis 2:7 NIV)**

The **second** thing God created in relation to man was his **soul**. The word *soul* or "psuche" (in New Testament Greek) is where we get the word "psyche" which basically means "being" or "person." This immaterial part of man is often referred to as "personality." The soul has features that are identifiable and different from the physical body.

The functions of the **soul** are the **intellect** or **mind, will**, and **emotions**. It is the **mind** that has the ability to gather, store, comprehend, analyze, and synthesize knowledge and information. Man has the ability to reason and think logically which sets him apart from the animal world. The **will** has the ability to make decisions. God created man with the ability to make moral choices. We call this ability "free moral agency." Man can choose right from wrong. Man is responsible for his choices. Our **emotions** allow us to appreciate God, His creation, and all human beings. So the **soul** consists of a person's Intellect—Will—Emotions.

The **third** thing God created in relation to man was his **spirit**. We have not only physical bodies and immaterial souls, but also immaterial *spirits.* We can act in ways that are significant in the spiritual realm of existence. We have immortality. We will not cease to live but will live forever. We can have a spiritual life enabling us to relate to God as persons. The *Holy Spirit* is God and is eternal and self-existent. The *human spirit* is created. God has created our spirit to allow us access to His person.

The first phase of God's plan to move us "from glory to glory" was to create a human personality in God's own image and consisting of a body-soul-spirit so He could communicate with us.

Stage 2: Redeemed Sons of God

The second phase of life's journey "from glory to glory" is that **created** sons of God are to become **redeemed** sons of God. Why was this necessary?

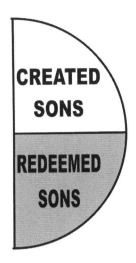

Something happened in the Garden of Eden between Adam and Eve and God. It affected the image of God in which they were created. Adam and Eve asserted their personalities apart from the will of God. God warned them:

> **But from the tree of the knowledge of good and evil you shall not eat, for in the day that you eat from it you shall surely die.**
>
> **(Genesis 2:17 NIV)**

Satan attacked Eve's mind and emotions and she disobeyed God. Adam disobeyed God by an act of his will. They both separated themselves from God by disobedience to God's request. The result was that God separated Himself from them. Immediately mankind was without a relationship with God. We all have inherited a nature that is now corrupted.

> **And it's clear enough, isn't it, that we're sinners, every one of us, in the same sinking boat with everyone else.**
>
> **(Romans 3:19)**

Since man sinned, he is certainly not as fully like God as he was before. His moral purity has been lost. His intellect is corrupted by falsehood. His relationships are often governed by selfishness. The image of God in which man was created has become distorted because of sin.

Nonetheless, it is encouraging to learn that redemption in Christ means we can have a new nature.

> **Your old life is dead. Your new life, which is your *real* life—even though invisible to spectators—is with Christ in God. *He* is your life.**
>
> **(Colossians 3:3)**

The goal for which God has redeemed us is that we might be conformed to the image of His Son and be exactly like Christ in our moral character. Jesus Christ made an agreement with His Heavenly Father to become a man, be our representative, and pay the penalty for our sin. The agreement was that He would come into the world as a man and live in perfect obedience to all the commands of the Father. This involved even obedience unto death on a cross. Paying the penalty for sin by His death, He would gather for Himself a people in order that none whom the Father had given Him would be lost.

After the fall in Genesis 3, the rest of Scripture is the story of God working out in history the amazing plan of redemption whereby sinful people could come into fellowship with God once again. The requirement for participation in this redemptive work is faith in Christ the Redeemer. This gift of grace is granted to all who put their faith in Jesus Christ as Savior and Lord. The promise of the blessings is the promise of eternal life.

> *Christ redeemed us from that self-defeating, cursed life by absorbing it completely into himself.*
>
> *(Galatians 3:13)*

Jesus becomes our life. By His resurrection we have eternal life. Jesus is eternal life!

> **Jesus said, "I am the Road, also the Truth, also the Life. No one gets to the Father apart from me.**
>
> **(John 14:6)**

Stage 3: Adopted Sons of God

The third phrase of our life's journey from glory to glory is realizing we are God's adopted sons.

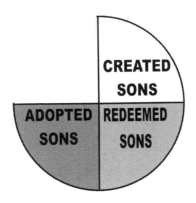

"We may define *adoption* as an act of God whereby he makes us members of his family."[5]

> God's Spirit touches our spirits and confirms who we really are. We know who he is, and we know who we are: Father and children. And we know we are going to get what's coming to us—an unbelievable inheritance! We go through exactly what Christ goes through. If we go through the hard times with him, then we're certainly going to go through the good times with him!
>
> (Romans 8:16-17)

What evidence do we see in our lives that we are God's children?

> Thus we have been set free to experience our rightful heritage. You can tell for sure that you are now fully adopted as his own children because God sent the Spirit of his Son into our lives crying out, "Papa! Father!" Doesn't that privilege of intimate conversation with God make it plain that you are not a slave, but a child? And if you are a child, you're also an heir, with complete access to the inheritance.
>
> (Galatians 4:5-7)

A birth relationship gives us the right to heirship, but participation in all that heirship means comes only to those who live according to the Will of the Father. There is much our Heavenly Father wishes to share with His *adopted* sons. He leads us through a thousand experiences. Experiences are like open doors through which we pass, each bringing growth and spiritual development.

One of the benefits that accompanies *adoption* is the way God relates to us. God relates to us as Father. He loves us, understands us, takes care of our needs, and gives us many good gifts. He gives us the gift of the Holy Spirit to comfort us and empower us for ministry. He also promises us a great inheritance in heaven because we have become joint heirs with Christ.

> **What a God we have! And how fortunate we are to have him, this Father of our Master Jesus! Because Jesus was raised from the dead, we've been given a brand-new life and have everything to live for, including a future in heaven and the future starts now! God is keeping careful watch over us and the future. The Day is coming when you'll have it all—life healed and whole.**

> **(I Peter 1:3-5)**

Stage 4: Glorified Sons of God

The final phase of the Father's Plan from glory to glory is the concept of glorification.

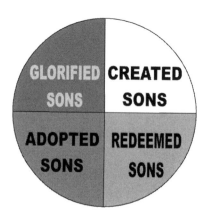

The stage in the application of redemption when we receive resurrected bodies is called *glorification*. The redemption of our bodies will occur when Christ returns and raises our bodies from the dead.

> **It stands to reason, doesn't it, that if the alive-and-present God who raised Jesus from the dead moves into your life, he'll do the same thing in you that he did in Jesus, bringing you alive to himself? When God lives and breathes in you (and he does, as surely as he did in Jesus), you are delivered from that dead life. With his Spirit living in you, your body will be as alive as Christ's!**
>
> **(Romans 8:10-11)**

When our bodies are raised from the dead and reunited with our souls, we will experience complete victory over the death that came as a result of the fall of Adam and Eve. Glorification is the final step in the application of redemption.

> **God knew what he was doing from the very beginning. He decided from the outset to shape the lives of those who love him along the same lines as the life of his Son. The Son stands first in the line of humanity he restored. We see the original and intended shape of our lives there in him. After God made that decision of what his children should be like, he followed it up by calling people by name. After he called them by name, he set them on a solid basis with himself. And then, after getting them established, he stayed with them to the end, gloriously completing what he had begun.**
>
> **(Romans 8:29-30)**

Not all Christians will die, but some who remain alive when Christ returns will simply have their bodies instantaneously changed into new, resurrected bodies that can never grow old or weak and can never die.

> **But let me tell you something wonderful, a mystery I'll probably never fully understand. We're not all going to die—*but* we are all going to be changed. You hear a blast**

to end all blasts from a trumpet, and in the time that you look up and blink your eyes—it's over. On signal from that trumpet from heaven, the dead will be up and out of their graves, beyond the reach of death, never to die again. At the same moment and in the same way, we'll all be changed. In the resurrection scheme of things, this has to happen: everything perishable taken off the shelves and replaced by the imperishable, this mortal replaced by the immortal. Then the saying will come true: Death swallowed by triumphant Life! Who got the last word, oh, Death? Oh, Death, who's afraid of you now?

(I Corinthians 15: 51-55)

We are God's masterpiece! He brings us from glory to glory.[6] Out of gratitude we can do nothing less than to live our lives for His glory! God's master plan is clearly laid out in summary form in Ephesians 1:3-14:

How blessed is God! And what a blessing he is! He's the Father of our Master, Jesus Christ, and takes us to the high places of blessings in him. Long before he laid down earth's foundations, he had us in mind, had settled on us as the focus of his love, to be made whole and holy by his love. Long, long ago he decided to adopt us into his family through Jesus Christ. (What pleasure he took in planning this!) He wanted us to enter into the celebration of his lavish gift-giving by the hand of his beloved Son.

Because of the sacrifice of the Messiah, his blood poured out on the altar of the Cross, we're a free people—free of penalties and punishment chalked up by all our misdeeds. And not just barely free, either. *Abundantly* free! He thought of everything, provided for everything we could possibly need, letting us in on the plans he took such delight in making. He set it all out before us in Christ, a long-range plan in which every—thing would be brought together and summed up in him, everything in deepest heaven, everything on planet earth.

It's in Christ that we find out who we are and what we are living for. Long before we first heard of Christ and got

our hopes up, he had his eye on us, had designs on us for glorious living, part of the overall purpose he is working out in everything and every one.

(Ephesians 1:3-12)

God's plan has been described in God's Word. We are to be His representatives while we are alive on earth. In the next lesson we will learn what God expects of us as His representatives.

Application

1. Why did God create man? *for his glory*
2. God made only one creature, *man* to be made in "the image of God."
3. What was the first thing God created in relation to man?
   body
4. Our *bodies* are the means by which we communicate with others.
5. The word *soul* means "being" or "person."
6. Our *mind, will nd emotions*, _____ are functions of the "soul.".
7. God created our *spirit* to allow us access to God's Person.
8. Redemption is necessary because sin distorted the *image god* in man and corrupted man's *nature*.
9. The goal of *redemption* is to conform us to the image of Jesus Christ.
10. *adoption* is an act of God whereby He makes us members of His family.
11. *glorification* for man takes place when we receive our resurrected bodies.
12. List the four stages of God's Plan for us:
    Created Sons of God
    Redeemed Sons of God
    Adopted Sons of God
    Glorified Sons of God

Assignment

Begin praying for someone you might begin discipling using Lesson 1.

CHAPTER THREE

THE GREAT COMMISSION:
Every Christian a Disciple-maker

But you are the ones chosen by God, chosen for the high calling of priestly work, chosen to be a holy people, God's instruments to do his work and speak out for him, to tell others of the night-and-day difference he made for you—from nothing to something, from rejected to accepted.

(I Peter 2:9-10)

Many Christians have a difficult time connecting Jesus' instructions for ministry to His disciples with instructions for us today. Often Christians engage in some form of ministry within or outside the church without a sound basis for their choice. If we want to make the best use of our time and efforts we have to use good judgment. We must have a clear understanding of Jesus' instructions to His disciples as found in The Great Commission. The Scripture teaches us that all believers are priests before God.

A. The Command

A recent survey of American adults found that only 25% of Christians could explain the meaning and purpose of the Great Commission.[7] Christianity is the only religion to have as its central theme the death and resurrection of Jesus. After His resurrection Jesus went back to heaven. Two years before His crucifixion, Jesus had made disciples of the twelve. He taught them about life in what He called, "The Kingdom of God."

A "disciple" is a student, learner, or pupil. The word "disciple" is sometimes used in a more specific way to indicate the twelve apostles of Jesus. In general, "disciples" refers to a larger group of those who believed that Jesus was the Christ, The Son of the Living God. They were "believers." As they were instructed in the teachings of Jesus, they became "disciples" of Jesus. These disciples were taught how to minister to others.

The reading of Matthew, Mark, Luke, and John reveals Jesus' plans for a company of followers to carry on his work. The disciples began to proclaim Christ as the resurrected Lord. Many in Jerusalem believed their message and a community of believers was formed. They were no longer a scattered group of disciples, but a commissioned, united New Testament Body, worshiping and waiting to be empowered with the Holy Spirit.

The work of Jesus did not end when He ascended into heaven. The Holy Spirit continued the work of Jesus in and through the Church. Jesus did not ascend until after He gave instructions through the Holy Spirit to His disciples. What is the believers' business here on earth?

And when the Holy Spirit comes on you, you will be able to be my witnesses in Jerusalem, all over Judea, and Samaria, even to the ends of the world.

(Acts 1:8)

Jerusalem $\longrightarrow$ Judea $\longrightarrow$ Samaria $\longrightarrow$ The ends of the World

Participation: Powerful but Explosive

Acts traces the early expansion of Christianity from its Jewish roots to a faith spread throughout the Roman Empire. The first key to understanding the Great Commission is that when Jesus returned to heaven, He sent the Holy Spirit to provide power to Christian disciples for Christian witnessing and Christian living. The Book of Acts is the story of the works of the Holy Spirit in and through the disciples of Jesus. The privilege of being Jesus' witness is given to every believer.

A careful consideration of the Great Commission as stated in Matthew's Gospel tells us how to make disciples and thus become disciple-makers.

God authorized and commanded me to commission you: Go out and train everyone you meet, far and near, in this way of life, marking them by baptism in the threefold name: Father, Son, and Holy Spirit. Then instruct them in the practice of all I have commanded you. I'll be with you as you do this, day after day after day, right up to the end of the age.

(Matthew 28:18-20)

Jesus met with His apostles on a mountain in Galilee. He told them to first of all "Go" and "make disciples." "Go" was an evangelistic command simply referring to bringing people to a saving faith in Jesus Christ. In order to accomplish this we must see all people as God sees them—as sinners.

Basically, all of us, whether insiders or outsiders, start out in identical conditions, which is to say that we all start out as sinners.

(Romans 3:9)

We are sinners by nature and by practice. We are to go out and share the good news: that is, forgiveness, hope, and love as found in Jesus Christ alone.

Coaching Personal Competence

The second part of the Great Commission is to "train everyone you meet." The Holy Spirit gave the apostles a body of truth to teach to these new believers. This body of truth is referred to in Acts 2 as "the teaching of the apostles." It was the apostles' doctrine that gave direction to everything that happened in the church in Jerusalem. The apostles were teaching what they had learned from Jesus Christ Himself. Each disciple is to coach another disciple to become competent in making disciples.

The third part of the Great Commission was to "baptize them in the name of the Father, the Son, and the Holy Spirit." Baptism marked them as Christ's disciples.

A proper understanding of the Great Commission is realizing that the object of the command was to "Make Disciples." The apostles were able to begin to duplicate this process through every member of the body of Jesus Christ.

The apostle Paul said to Timothy,

> **So, my son, throw yourself into the work for Christ. Pass on what you heard from me—the whole congregation saying Amen!—to reliable leaders who are competent to teach others.**

> **(2 Timothy 2:1-2)**

The subject of the Great Commission is that every disciple is commanded to make other disciples. This is not an option but a command. The growth of the Kingdom of God is only accomplished by Jesus' method of disciple-making. This is a four-step process:

1. Our ministry must depend on the Holy Spirit.
2. We must prepare ourselves to "Go" and explain the Gospel to unbelievers. There is no other way for them to become disciples of Jesus.
3. Those who receive Jesus Christ as their Savior and Lord are to be "baptized" as a profession of their faith.
4. They are to be "instructed" for a measure of time with the principles of Christian living that result in their becoming disciple-makers themselves.

So what is to be the primary ministry of every believer? Jesus' disciples would receive power after the Holy Spirit came upon them. Through the Spirit's power their business would be to serve as Christ's witnesses, telling what they had seen, heard, and experienced. Beginning at Jerusalem they would carry their witness through Judea, Samaria, and then to the ends of the earth. Christians today are commanded to do the same. God loved us so much that He died for our sin. By faith we received His free gift of eternal life, which is the Good News called the Gospel. Disciple-making does not stop, however, with the introducing of unbelievers to Jesus Christ. A new believer is like a newborn baby. He cannot fend for himself. We must continue to build basic Christian principles into the lives of new believers.

Many have come to that beginning point of salvation. They are believers. But some have not begun to follow Him as Lord. The result is that they have not had the delight of making disciples. "The progression is: a believer, a follower, a disciple. A disciple is a believer who has become a follower of Jesus and obedient to His methods of disciple-making."[8]

Can you locate yourself in one of these categories? Check one.

Believer _____ Follower _____ Disciple _____

Christians do not need to fail. The coming of the Spirit is an empowering experience. Jesus emphasized that His followers could not wait for ideal conditions before spreading the gospel to the nations. He told them that this age, and especially the end times, would be characterized by wars, rumors of wars, famines, and earthquakes.

> **When reports come in of wars and rumored wars, keep your head and don't panic. This is routine history; this is no sign of the end. Nation will fight nation and ruler fight ruler, over and over. Famines and earthquakes will occur in various places. This is nothing compared to what is coming.**
>
> **(Matthew 24:6-8)**

Disciples of Jesus must spread the gospel to all nations despite all these natural calamities and political upheavals. How would this be possible? Jesus promised they would receive power as a result of being filled with His

Spirit. This would be the secret of success in the Church Age until its final consummation when Jesus returns.

> **We teach in a spirit of profound common sense so that we can bring each person to maturity**
>
> **(Colossians 1:28)**

These Twelve Essentials of Disciple-making which you are learning will help you become the person God wants you to be. Your experience of being discipled by a disciple-maker will help you know how to disciple someone else. The Great Commission informs us that we are to disciple everyone who has not been discipled. We can help other Christians to mature by encouraging them to become disciple-makers. This is a fulfilling ministry and is a command given to us by Jesus Himself: **MAKE DISCIPLES!**

> **Our firm decision is to work from this focused center: One man died for everyone. That puts everyone in the same boat. He included everyone in his death so that everyone could also be included in his life, a resurrection life, a far better life than people ever lived on their own.**
>
> **(2 Corinthians 5:17-20)**

B. The Crisis

From the beginning the disciples preached the resurrection of Jesus. On the Day of Pentecost the apostle Peter preached telling those in attendance to repent and be baptized in the name of Jesus.

> **Change your life. Turn to God and be baptized, each of you, in the name of Jesus Christ, so your sins are forgiven. Receive the gift of the Holy Spirit**
>
> **(Acts 2:38)**

Many accepted Peter's invitation. They were baptized and about three thousand were added to the Jesus movement that day. That is how the Christian church started. It was quite a beginning. The first forty years saw the infant church spread at a phenomenal rate. It sprang up in most major cities in the Roman Empire and was transformed into a fellowship of many different peoples. The disciples called their new movement "The Way." They meant by it a gathering of God's people.

The Apostle Paul's converts were a mixed lot. He was concerned about instilling Christian principles in those who gathered to worship Jesus Christ. He established churches by making disciples. He called unbelievers to repentance and instructed them in the teachings of the apostles.

For practical purposes A.D. 70 and the destruction of Jerusalem mark the end of the apostolic period. Most of the original apostles were dead, and the churches they had founded had passed into new hands. In the period that followed, Christianity spread throughout the Roman Empire. Christians realized that they were a part of a rapidly expanding movement. They called it "catholic," suggesting that it was universal.

The early Church grew because everyone was witnessing to others and they were making disciples of the new believers. Following Pentecost everyone was in awe because the believers lived in a wonderful harmony. They understood the need for relationships. Everyone was making disciples of someone else. Christianity was a spiritual explosion. The disciples had a spiritual vision and a conviction that all believers should be making disciple-makers.

> **They followed a daily discipline of worship in the Temple followed by meals at home, every meal a celebration, exuberant and joyful, as they praised God. People in general liked what they saw. Every day their numbers grew as God added those who were saved.**
>
> **(Acts 2:46-47)**

What was the crisis? "The Christians began to lose their vision and ignored Jesus' command to fulfill the Great Commission. No one seems to know just how the single pastor, assisted by the elders and deacons, became the widespread pattern within the churches, but we know it did. Before long, instead of being empowered by the Holy Spirit, they relied on the clergy to do the work of ministry."[9]

To face the challenges of their times the Christians turned increasingly to their bishops for spiritual leadership. By the late second century the unchallenged leader in church affairs was the bishop. These changes in the structure and functioning of the church created institutionalism that has devastated the Church to this day. In the first and second centuries, Christians looked for proof of the Spirit's power not in an office, but in the lives of believers. The Apostle Paul described the Spirit's work in terms of the edification of the entire church. This edification means growth in all that is good.

> **But what happens when we live God's way? He brings gifts into our lives, much the same way that fruit appears in an orchard—things like affection for others, exuberance about life, serenity. We develop a willingness to stick with things, a sense of compassion in the heart, and a conviction that a basic holiness permeates things and people. We find ourselves involved in loyal commitments.**
>
> **(Galatians 5:22-23)**

Effective disciple-making means every believer is to be a witness to unbelievers and disciple them until they are mature enough to disciple others and in turn fulfill the Great Commission. Warren Wiersbe in his *Bible Exposition Commentary* points out the necessity of disciple-making. "In many respects, we have departed from this pattern. In most churches, the congregation pays the pastor to preach, win the lost, and build up the saved—while the church members function as cheerleaders (if they are enthusiastic) or spectators. The 'converts' are won, baptized, and given the right hand of fellowship, then they join the other spectators. How much faster our churches would grow, and how much stronger and happier our church members would be, if each one were discipling another believer. The only way a local church can 'be fruitful and multiply' instead of growing by 'addition' is with a systematic discipleship program."[10]

We must get back to disciple-making. It is not an option; it is a command and the responsibility of every believer.

C. The Context

The strategy of disciple-making, as a spiritual reproductive process, begins with our dependence on The Holy Spirit to lead us within the sphere of our life context to share our life experiences with those around us. Discipleship declines when we refuse to accept the ministry God has called us to perform. Steven Collins, in *Christian Discipleship, says* "based on the number of church—goers it takes 50 to 500 Christians to produce one convert in a year's time."[11]

The Great Commission—**"GO"**—is directed personally to you. If you are a disciple of Jesus, you have the responsibility to fulfill your part and become a disciple-maker.

Developing meaningful contacts

Where do you go? As a disciple-maker, you are Jesus' personal representative to those within your life-context. You minister within your sphere of influence.

> **Our firm decision is to work from this focused center: One man died for everyone. That puts everyone in the same boat. He included everyone in his death so that everyone could also be included in his life, a resurrection life, a far better life than people ever lived on their own.**
>
> **Because of this decision we don't evaluate people by what they have or how they look. We looked at the Messiah that way once and got it all wrong, as you know. We certainly don't look at him that way anymore. Now we look inside, and what we see is that anyone united with the Messiah gets a fresh start, is created new. The old life is gone; a new life burgeons! Look at it! All this comes from the God who settled the relationship between us and him, and then called us to settle our relationships with each other. God put the world square with himself through the Messiah, giving the world a fresh start by offering forgiveness of sins. God has given us the task of telling everyone what he is doing. We're Christ's representatives. God uses us to persuade men and women to drop their differences and enter into God's work of making things right between them. We're speaking for Christ himself now: Become friends with God; he's already a friend with you.**
>
> **(2 Corinthians 5:14-20)**

Family → Friends → Community → City

The most responsible action we can take toward our generation is life-style evangelism. A good place to start is with your family. Target those at work only when it is appropriate. Develop social contacts. Volunteer for community projects. Those with whom you do business are good prospects. Go to people you know, people you use to know, and people you would like to know. Many who attend your church likely have never been discipled. Trust God to bring across your path in life people you can disciple. He will bring people that you would never have expected.

"Many of us have such limited opportunity to witness because we have fewer non-Christian friends. As important as our ministry within the church may be, it is just as important to have fellowship with those outside the church. They are the ones who need our friendship and God's forgiveness. We must go where non-Christians are. We need to have disciples out into every area of our community."[12]

Do it because it is the right thing to do

Disciple-making works wherever there are people. Political systems have tried to stop the growth of the Church, but the Church has been triumphant. Disciple-making is relevant in every culture. Disciple-making is a timeless principle. It worked in the first century and it will work in the twenty-first century. Throughout the history of the Church disciple-making has been effective among the poor, the wealthy, the uneducated, and the intellectuals. Disciple-making has been tried and proven as the most effective method for building the Kingdom of God.

You are competent to coach others and in turn fulfill your part of the Great Commission.

Application

1. A _disciple_ is a student, a learner, or a pupil.
2. What is the disciple's business?

    a. _witnes_
    b. _disciple maker_

3. What are the four steps to becoming a disciple-maker?

    a. _depend on the holy spirit_
    b. _Go nd explain the gospel_
    c. _encourage new comers to be baptized_
    d. _teach new believers basic principles_

4. The Great Commission is not an _option_ but a _command_.
5. After 70 A.D. the early church was called _Catholic_, meaning "universal."
6. The crisis in the Church after the second century was: (Circle the correct answer.)

    a. The laity lost its vision for the ministry.
    b. The clergy took over the ministry.
    c. The Great Commission was disobeyed by many.
    d. All of the above.

7. Where does a disciple go to make contacts? Your sphere of _influence_.
8. You are a _minister_ of God.

Assignment

1. Ask God to bring to your attention someone's name (a relative, friend, neighbor, associate, business contact, social contact) and begin praying for an opportunity to share with that person what God has done in changing your life.
2. Have you found someone to disciple?

CHAPTER FOUR

BIBLE STUDY: A Method of Bible Study

Everybody should love the Bible because it gives us the answers to the purpose and meaning of life. The Bible is the record of God's dealing with mankind. The Bible traces how God has revealed Himself down through history. We cannot become effective disciple-makers without learning how to study the Bible.

What is the Bible?

The Bible is a collection of sixty-six books that were written over a period of more than 1,500 years. More than forty different people wrote the various books of the Bible. Among them were kings, prophets, teachers, farmers, poets, priests, statesmen, philosophers, fishermen, sheepherders, doctors, and a tax collector. They wrote stories, poems, histories, prophecies, proverbs, biographies, and letters. The Bible is about real people and about the God who is real.

The Bible is divided into two parts: the Old Testament containing thirty-nine books and the New Testament consisting of twenty-seven. The Old Testament was written before the time of Christ. It shows us the sinfulness of mankind and it looks forward to the coming of Jesus, the Messiah or the Christ, who will save us from our sin. The New Testament tells us of the entrance of God into the world in the person of Jesus Christ. It tells how Jesus provided Salvation for you and me from our sin by His death and resurrection. It also describes the founding and growth of Christianity in the first century A.D. The Bible is one of the means through which the Holy Spirit works to convey blessings into the life of the believer.

God directed the production of the Bible by the process of "inspiration."

Every part of Scripture is God-breathed and useful one way or another—showing us truth, exposing our rebellion, correcting our mistakes, training us to live God's way. Through the Word we are put together and shaped up for the tasks God has for us.

(2 Timothy 3:15-17)

The word "inspiration" means "God breathed." "It is a technical term for the Holy Spirit's supernatural guidance of those who received special revelation from God as they wrote the books of the Bible."[13] Although the authors were human beings, God breathed into them His thoughts to be written down and preserved. The human writers did not merely write their own opinions; their words were inspired by God. God breathed out the Bible. The Bible is the Word of God.

In a careful study of the Bible we notice that each human author has his own peculiar literary style, vocabulary, and special emphasis. The Bible is a collection of literature and it is a masterpiece. The Bible contains the greatest ethical system found today. The history found in the Bible has been confirmed by both historical investigation and archaeology. The deepest gnawing within the human heart is for adequate answers to the purpose and meaning of life. It was the intention of God the Father that mankind might find the answers to life's deepest problems.

Everybody should read the Bible

You may have noticed by now that you have been reading many Bible verses as you have gone along in this study. This has been done intentionally. It is important that you establish the habit of Bible reading. Christian people talk about the Bible, defend the Bible, and even exalt the Bible, but many Christians seldom look into the Bible. We read newspapers, magazines, novels, and all kinds of books; we listen to the radio and watch television by the hours. But the time spent reading the Bible among Christians is appallingly small. The great preacher Charles Spurgeon said, "The Bible to many is God's unopened letter." The Bible should be the book we live by. Bible reading is the means by which we learn. Our lives are the product of our thoughts. To live right we need to think right. We need to read the Bible regularly so God's thoughts become our thoughts. Bible reading is the most effective character-forming power we know. Every Christian, young and old, should be a faithful reader of the Bible.

> **It takes more than bread to stay alive. It takes a steady stream of words from God's mouth.**
>
> **(Matthew 4:4)**

How do we know the Bible is true? Because it is logically consistent and coherent. It tells us where we came from, where we are going, and how to get there. The theme of the Bible is that human beings exist for the purpose of pleasing God the Father. The Father's purpose in creating us is so that we might live our lives to please Him. How do we please God the Father? This is accomplished by allowing God the Father, through the Son, Jesus Christ, to live in us and express Himself through us to others. The purpose of the Father is to have a vast family of sons and daughters (who are just like His unique Son, Jesus Christ) through whom He can express Himself. If we are going to understand God's Word, then we must make time to read the Bible.

Read the Bible with an open heart and mind. Bible reading is a part of life- changing discipleship. You may want to consider your daily devotional reading in *The Living Bible* or *The International Standard Bible* for easier reading.

Let's learn how to study the Bible.

The purpose of studying the Bible is the total transformation of the person.

The apostle Paul tells us that we are transformed through the renewal of the mind.

> So here's what I want you to do, God helping you: Take your everyday, ordinary life—your sleeping, eating, going-to-work, and walking around life—and place it before God as an offering. Embracing what God does for you is the best thing you can do for him. Don't become so well-adjusted to your culture that you fit into it without even thinking. Instead, fix your attention on God. You'll be changed from the inside out. Readily recognize what he wants from you, and quickly respond to it. Unlike the culture around you, always dragging you down to its level of immaturity, God brings the best out of you, develops well-formed maturity in you.
>
> (Romans 12:1-2)

The mind is renewed by applying it to those things that will transform it.

> Summing it all up, friends, I'd say you'll do best by filling your minds and meditating on things true, noble, reputable, authentic, compelling, gracious—the best, not the worst; the beautiful, not the ugly; things to praise, not things to curse. Put into practice what you learned from me, what you heard and saw and realized. Do that, and God, who makes everything work together, will work you into his most excellent harmonies.
>
> (Philippians 3:8-9)

Jesus made it unmistakably clear that the knowledge of truth will set us free.

> Then you will experience for yourselves the truth, and the truth will free you.
>
> (John 8:32)

Paul urges us to focus on things that are true, honorable, just, pure, lovely, and gracious. This is why we study the Bible. There are **four basic steps in studying the Bible** that may be helpful:

1. *Humility.* Study simply cannot happen until we are willing to be subject to the subject matter. We must come as a student.
2. *Understanding.* As we read the Bible we must understand what the author is saying.
3. *Interpretation.* We must ask what the author means.
4. *Application.* How do I apply this truth to my life?

The four basic functions for applying the Word of God to our daily walk are mentioned in 2 Timothy 3:15-16

> **Every part of Scripture is God-breathed and useful one way or another—showing us truth, exposing our rebellion, correcting our mistakes, training us to live God's way.**

Now it is time for a little Bible study. Let's look at Romans 12:1-2 and follow the steps mentioned above.

The first step is **humility**. We are going to take a few minutes and pray, asking God to help us submit to the truth He wants us to learn . The second step is **understanding**. We must ask "what is the author saying?" We can determine this by asking questions.

Who wrote this? (Read Romans 1:1)

> **I, Paul, am a devoted slave of Jesus Christ on assignment, authorized as an apostle to proclaim God's words and acts.**

To whom did Paul write this? (Read Romans 1:1)

> **I write this letter to all the Christians in Rome, God's friends.**

What is the subject of Romans 12:1-2?

(Write a title for this passage.)

_____

Example: Place your life before God.

The third step is **interpretation**. What does it mean? What does it mean to place your life before God?

(Summarize this passage in your own words.)

_____

_____

_____

_____

Example: Take everything you are, and everything you do, everyday and place it before God as an offering. Accept everything God does for you. Don't accept everything in your culture without first thinking it through. Fix your attention on God. Allow God to change you from the inside out. Quickly respond to what God wants from you. Do not allow your culture to drag you down to levels of immaturity. God will bring the best out of you.

The fourth step is **application**. We look for:

1. What truths do I need to learn?
   (Example: That every part of my body, everything I think, and everything I do are to be under God's control)
2. What rebellion do I have in submitting to the truth?
   (List any areas in your life that are not under God's control.)

_____

_____

(Examples: Things that you see, hear, and do that would displease God. Things that you think or attitudes you hold that are unhealthy. Decisions you make that are selfish.)

3. What mistakes have I made that need to be corrected.
   (List the mistakes you have made that need correction.)

_____

_____

(Examples: I have omitted reading the Bible. I make decisions without consulting God first. I seek advice from ungodly people. I have put myself above others including my spouse.)

Now write down what you are going to do about each one.

_____

_____

_____

4. What do I need to learn concerning God's Ways? (List any areas where you believe you need help in learning about God's Will for you.)

_____

_____

_____

(Examples: I do not understand how to determine God's purpose in life. I do not know my responsibilities to God in the wisest use of my finances. How do I handle my anger? How can I become a more loving person? How can I serve God best?)

Reading and studying God's Word are the ways we grow in our life-changing discipleship pursuit.

Some basic tools to help you study the Bible

As you study the Bible, don't underestimate yourself. The Bible is not a complex database that requires skilled technicians to unlock it. The spirit in which you approach the Bible is more important than your ability to use Bible study tools. However, the following basic tools will help you study:

. . . *a good Study Bible*, the complete Bible with notes and other helpful materials added (maps, introductions to each book and cross references to other Scriptures.)

. . . *a Bible handbook* provides background before you read through a book of the Bible and gives you explanations and illustrations as you read.

. . . *a Bible dictionary* will help you read the Bible with understanding because it gives you information about people, places, words, and events in the Bible.

. . . *Bible Study Software*. The invention of the computer revolutionized Bible study. Whole libraries of Bible study books are available on CD. Software allows you to locate information instantaneously.

. . . *a notebook*. Keep a notebook by your side to preserve your thoughts, observations, and your special applications. The notes you make while studying the Bible make good material to pray into your life for spiritual growth.

Application

1. The Bible consists of how many Books?
   _____Sixty Six_____

2. Name the two parts of the Bible.
   _____Old nd New testaments_____

3. The _Old testament_ reveals the sinfulness of mankind and looks forward to the coming of Jesus.

4. The _New testament_ tells of the entrance of God into the world in the person of Jesus Christ. .

5. The word "inspiration" means _God breathed_

6. The _Bible_ is the Word of God.

7. Who should read the Bible? _everyone_

8. The most effective character-forming power we know is:
   _____reading_____

9. The purpose of studying the Bible is the total _transformation_ of the person.

10. What are the four basic steps in studying the Bible?
    _____humility_____
    _____Understanding_____
    _____Interpretation_____
    _____application_____

Assignment

1. Pray for someone to disciple and then teach them Lesson One.

2. Choose a short passage of Scripture and practice the principles outlined in this chapter.

CHAPTER FIVE

EFFECTIVE PRAYING: Praying with Results

A commitment to the Word of God and to prayer are inseparable priorities. As the disciples watched Jesus in action, they learned that He spent much time in prayer. Prayer is the key to fruitfulness in our ministry.

> **So if you're serious about living this new resurrection life with Christ, *act* like it. Pursue the things over which Christ presides. Don't shuffle along, eyes to the ground, absorbed with the things right in front of you. Look up, and be alert to what is going on around Christ—that's where the action is. See things from *his* perspective.**
>
> **(Colossians 3:1-2)**

What is prayer?

Jesus is the centerpiece of everything we believe. We are God's house; Jesus Christ is in charge of the house. Our main task is to live in responsive obedience to God's action revealed in Jesus. Our part of the action is the act of faith in what He says. Prayer is communication with God. Prayer is the privilege of access to God. Prayer must be learned, and the Holy Spirit is the teacher.

The Bible is God's love letter to us. Prayer is God's direct line for our communicating with Him. Prayer is our conscious experience of God's presence. Prayer is the union of our thoughts with the will of God. Prayer is our communicating our thoughts and desires to God. However, prayer is **not** God yielding to our selfish petitions.

Prayer is simply the communication tool for talking to God and listening to God speak.

> **God means what he says. What he says goes. His powerful Word is sharp as a surgeon's scalpel, cutting through everything, whether doubt or defense, laying us open to listen and obey. Nothing and no one is impervious to God's Word. We can't get away from it—no matter what. Now that we know what we have—Jesus, this great High Priest with ready access to God—let's not let it slip through our fingers. We don't have a priest who is out of touch with our reality. He's been through weakness and testing, experienced it all—all but the sin. So let's walk right up to him and get what he is so ready to give. Take the mercy, accept the help.**
>
> **(Hebrews 4:12-16)**

Prayer, therefore, is two-way communicating with God. Prayer's primary purpose is to grow a relationship with God. Prayer is the avenue for us to know God personally. If we read the Bible and listen to others tell us about God, but we never talk to God ourselves, we do not have a real relationship with God. Prayer releases God's will on earth. God decreed that certain aspects of His will would only be released with prayer.

Prayer is so important that we should ponder questions like:

. . . What blessings are not falling on my family because of my lack of prayer?

. . . What spiritual blessings are *not* occurring in my church because of my lack of prayer?

. . . What darkness is not being penetrated in the world because of my lack of prayer?

The acrostic ACTS is an aid to prayer

We talk to God through prayer. A helpful tool in learning to pray effectively is the acrostic A-C-T-S. Each letter in the acrostic indicates a vital element of prayer.

A= Adoration
C= Confession
T= Thanksgiving
S= Supplication

Adoration. In prayer we express our reverence and praise as we celebrate our life in Christ. In prayer we must always remember to whom we are speaking. Prayer is to be addressed to God alone. People praying to God's creation or to human beings is idolatry. God listens to those who approach Him with sincerity. I had the privilege of attending a Christian college. Every class began with the students standing and repeating the Lord's Prayer. It was repeated as if they were having a contest to see who could say it the fastest. You could not understand what was being said, and it was more of a mockery than a simple, meaningful prayer to God. Empty and insincere phrases are an offense against God. Adoration is respect for God and praise for who He is.

Confession. The most important prayer you ever prayed was a prayer for salvation. We must approach God in humility. We must remember who He is, but also who and what we are. We are sinful creatures. We are His adopted children. We only have the right to approach Him because of what Jesus Christ did for us on the cross. Then God invites us to come boldly before Him. We humbly confess our sins to Him, and He grants to us His forgiveness. Confession is coming to God and saying, "I need help." We all have needs that must be prayed for in our marriage, business, studies, or relationships. God wants to help us. We all need help at one time or another, so don't be too proud to ask for it.

Thanksgiving. We receive joyful hearts, peace of mind, and victory over sin when we accept God's forgiveness. We cannot forgive our own sin. We should have a thankful heart for God's mercy and grace. God is always there for us. It is good to thank God for the blessings He sends to us in the past, now, and in the future. Thanksgiving is a vital part of prayer.

Supplication. Supplication takes on two district forms: prayers for others and prayer for ourselves. God calls us to pray for others: family, friends, neighbors, God's servants around the world, and our enemies. In more than fifty years of ministry I have prayed for thousands of people in hospital beds. I have prayed at funerals for families who have lost their loved ones. I have witnessed people who were delivered from circumstances that would have brought them into harm's way. God *does* answer prayer. We are also instructed not to worry but to bring our desires, plans, needs, and even wants to Him in prayer.

How Can I Learn to Pray?

The "Five Finger Prayer Method" is an easy way to remember what to pray for. Your *thumb* is nearest you. So begin your prayers by praying for those closest to you. They are the easiest to remember. To pray for our loved ones is, as C.S. Lewis once said, a "sweet duty."

The next finger is the *pointing finger*. Pray for those who teach, instruct, and heal. This indicates teachers, doctors, and ministers. They need support and wisdom in pointing others in the right direction. Keep them in your prayers.

The *middle finger* is the tallest finger. It reminds us of our leaders. Pray for the president, leaders in business and industry, and administrators. These people shape our nation and guide public opinion. They need God's guidance.

The *fourth finger* is our ring finger. Surprising to many is the fact that this is our weakest finger, as any piano teacher will testify. It should remind us to pray for those who are weak, in trouble or in pain. They need our prayers day and night. You cannot pray too much for them.

And lastly comes our *little finger*, the smallest finger of all which is where we should place ourselves in relation to God and others. As the Bible says, "The least shall be the greatest among you." (Luke 9:48) Your pinkie should remind you to pray for yourself. By the time you have prayed for the other four groups, your own needs will be put into proper perspective and you will be able to pray for yourself more effectively.

> **Don't fret or worry. Instead of worrying, pray. Let petitions and praises shape your worries into prayers, letting God know your concerns. Before you know it, a sense of God's wholeness, everything coming together for good, will come and settle you down. It's wonderful what happens when Christ displaces worry at the center of your life.**
>
> **(Philippians 4:6-7)**

Jesus instructs His disciples how to pray

Jesus gave instructions about prayer and taught His disciples how to pray. He taught them to pray to God with simplicity:

> **And when you come before God, don't turn that into a theatrical production either. All these people making a regular show out of their prayers, hoping for stardom! Do you think God sits in a box seat?**
>
> **Here's what I want you to do: Find a quiet, secluded place so you won't be tempted to role-play before God. Just be there as simply and honestly as you can manage. The focus will shift from you to God, and you will begin to sense his grace.**
>
> **The world is full of so-called prayer warriors who are prayer-ignorant. They're full of formulas and programs and advice, peddling techniques for getting what you want from God. Don't fall for that nonsense. This is your Father you are dealing with, and he knows better than you what you need.**

With a God like this loving you, you can pray very simply. Like this:

> Our Father in heaven,
> Reveal who you are.
> Set the world right;
> Do what's best—
> as above, so below.

> Keep us alive with three square meals. Keep us forgiven with you and forgiving others. Keep us safe from ourselves and the Devil. You're in charge!
> You can do anything you want! You're ablaze in beauty!

> Yes. Yes. Yes.

> (Matthew 6:5-13)

We pray in the name of Jesus because we do acknowledge His office as mediator. He is our High Priest. Christ is our intercessor and the Holy Spirit is our helper in prayer. The prayer in faith is a prayer trusting in God's wisdom and kindness.

> The first thing I want you to do is pray. Pray every way you know how, for everyone you know. Pray especially for rulers and their governments to rule well so we can be quietly about our business of living simply, in humble contemplation. This is the way our Savior God wants us to live.

> (I Timothy 2:1-3)

How to draw near to God

We do not naturally delight in drawing near to God. We pay lip service to the power of prayer. We call it indispensable. We know the Scriptures call for it. Yet we fail to pray. Mastering the art of prayer takes time. The time we give to it will be a measure of its importance to us. We always find time for the things that are the most important to us. We cannot learn about prayer except by praying. It is prayer that brings us into a closer fellowship with God.

Are we ready to pray? Let's take a little self-test!

Here is a quick checklist. Place a circle around the check if you can answer YES!

- ✓ Are all your sins confessed?
- ✓ Are all relationships with others made right?
- ✓ Are you seeking God's Will in all things?
- ✓ Are you seeking to glorify God above all things?
- ✓ Are you depending on the Holy Spirit's guidance for your life?
- ✓ Are you trusting God in spite of what seems to be?
- ✓ Will you praise God no matter what?

When we look at the life of Jesus, we see that prayer was the dominant feature. He spent full nights in prayer. He rose before dawn to talk with His Father. When He had to face a crisis, Jesus prayed specifically, adding "Not my will but thine be done."

The Helper in Our Praying

We are to pray in the power and energy of the Spirit. All the human energy of heart, mind, and will can achieve great human results, but praying in the Holy Spirit releases supernatural resources. The Spirit delights in helping us pray. Sometimes the ignorance of our minds hinders our prayers. The Spirit knows the mind of God and shares that knowledge with us as we wait and listen. God's voice may come in the form of an idea. It may come from a letter we have received, or a telephone call from someone who cares and gives us encouragement. Also, we can hear God's voice when we read the Bible.

A word of caution!! In recent days I have listened to a host of television evangelists who each make the claim of God speaking audibly to them about a number of people in the audience who were to send them "X" number of dollars and they were to do it immediately. My word of caution is to be very careful when listening to those who say, "God told me to tell you this," as if God is not capable of telling you Himself.

There have been times in the Bible when God has **audibly** spoken to people. God the Father spoke to Jesus three times and to the apostle Paul once. God NEVER spoke audibly about money. Anytime I hear someone say, "The Lord audibly told me to do this," I immediately run—because this is the way human beings get people to acquiesce to what *they* want, not what *God* wants.

The principle way God speaks to us is through His written Word. We can know the will of God concerning the prayers we make. Our capacity to know God's will is the basis for all prayers of faith. God speaks to us clearly through our mind and heart. The Bible instructs us directly concerning the will of God on all matters of principle.

The Holy Spirit instructs us in the will of God. It is honoring to God when our first response to any situation is to consult Him. It is better to make prayer our *first* choice not our *last*. Prayer is not a last resort for one to use in times of crisis. Prayer will keep us *out* of the crises.

> **Meanwhile, the moment we get tired in the waiting, God's Spirit is right alongside helping us along. If we don't know how or what to pray, it doesn't matter. He does our praying in and for us, making prayer out of our wordless sighs, our aching groans. He knows us far better than we know ourselves, knows our pregnant condition, and keeps us present before God. That's why we can be so sure that every detail in our lives of love for God is worked into something good.**
>
> **(Romans 8:26-28)**

How does God answer prayer?

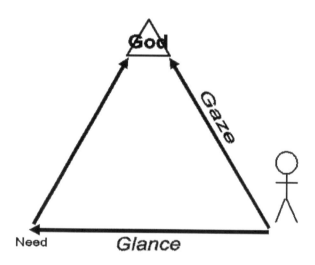

"Let your gaze be on God. Ask him to interpret any situation from his viewpoint and to tell us what he wants done. It is then we can pray with conviction about any situation because our prayer is based on the known will of God. Then, let your glance be on your request. If we allow our gaze to be on our request, it will dominate our prayers; we will tell God what we see and what needs to be done."[14]

> **If God gives such attention to the appearance of wildflowers—most of which are never even seen—don't you think he'll attend to you, take pride in you, do his best for you? What I'm trying to do here is to get you to relax, to not be so preoccupied with *getting*, so you can respond to God's *giving*. People who don't know God and the way he works fuss over these things, but you know both God and how he works. Steep your life in God-reality, God-initiative, God provisions. Don't worry about missing out. You'll find all your everyday human concerns will be met.**
>
> **(Matthew 6:30-33)**

When God lays a burden on our hearts and we keep praying for an answer, it is obvious He intends to grant an answer. God answers prayer basically in one of three ways:

a. When our prayers are within the Will of God, He answers *Yes*.
b. When our prayers are outside God's Will, He answers *No*.
c. When granting an answer, but the timing is not right, He tells us to *Wait*.

Why doesn't God Answer My Prayer?

The Bible is very clear on the reasons why prayers go unanswered. God will not cooperate with prayers of mere self-interest. Nor will He answer prayers from impure motives. God's ear is closed to people who cling to their sins. Maturity is not how long we have been a Christian, but how fast we get on our knees when we know we have sinned. God does not tolerate unbelief. In all our prayers the motive must be to please God.

What can we expect when we make prayer a priority? We can expect God to bring us to the end of ourselves, become more Christ-like, and become confident in all we do. There is no doubt about it. Meaningful communication with God should become natural, important, and enjoyable. God has something personal to say to you each day. Jesus' disciples understood that life-changing discipleship means that prayer is what disciples need most to be effective.

Samuel Chadwick said, "though a man shall have all knowledge about prayer, and though he understands all mysteries about prayer, unless he prays, he will never learn to pray."

Application

1. Prayer is a _____ communication with God. It is our expression of our desire to do the Will of God, and God's expression to us communicating what His Will is for us.
2. The acrostic ACTS is an aid to prayer. Each letter indicates a vital element of prayer.

    _____—reverence and praise.

    _____—coming to God and saying, "I need help."

    _____—A spirit of appreciation for God's mercy and grace.

    _____—prayer for others and prayer for ourselves.
3. Jesus taught His disciples to pray with _____,

    addressed to _____.

    and to pray in _____.
4. How do we draw near to God?

    a. Spend _____ in prayer.

    b. Pray _____

    c. Pray according to the _____

    d. Pray in the _____

5. What are the three ways God answers prayer?

    a. _____

    b. _____

    c. _____

Assignment

Begin a daily time of Bible study and prayer.

CHAPTER SIX

THE WORK OF THE HOLY SPIRIT:
Controlled by the Holy Spirit

When you were physically born, you came into this life naked and became a member of your physical family. Your mother began to feed you and clothe you. Those who believe and receive Christ are born into the family of God. Believing and receiving Jesus is just like being born a second time. This is why our experience is called New Birth. This New Birth is a spiritual birth and is a work of God himself. It does not come through human effort, but rather it is something that God does in us.

> **What a God we have! And how fortunate we are to have him, this Father of our Master Jesus! Because Jesus was raised from the dead, we've been given a brand-new life and have everything to live for, including a future in heaven—and the future starts now!**

> **(I Peter 1:3)**

Because we are God's children He begins to feed us and clothe us through his Word, prayer, and by the Holy Spirit. It is important to know that every child of God has been born again by the Holy Spirit.

Who is the Holy Spirit?

The Bible clearly teaches that the Holy Spirit is the third person in the Godhead: God the Father, God the Son, and God the Holy Spirit. There is only one God, but within the Godhead there are three personalities. This is often referred to as the Trinity.

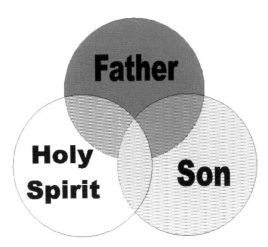

This diagram describes a relationship of one God who is three persons. It is possible for us to enjoy a personal relationship with the Holy Spirit because He is a distinct person. Before the Lord Jesus Christ went up into heaven, He promised to send His followers a New Companion. The Holy Spirit is now in the world in Jesus' place. All those who have received Jesus and are children of God have the Holy Spirit in their lives.

How does the Holy Spirit clothe us with Christ?

The Holy Spirit helps us to properly understand God's Word.

> **No one's ever seen or heard anything like this, Never so much as imagined anything quite like it—What God has arranged for those who love him. But *you've* seen and heard it because God by his Spirit has brought it all out into the open before you. The Spirit, not content to flit around on the surface, dives into the depths of God, and brings out what God planned all along. Who ever knows what you are thinking and planning except you yourself? The same with God—except that he not only knows what he's thinking, but he lets *us* in on it.**

> **(I Corinthians 2:9-11)**

The Holy Spirit joins Himself with our spirit restoring our relationship with God. By receiving the Holy Spirit into our lives we are sealed or given God's mark of ownership. We belong to Him. The Holy Spirit places us into the Body of Christ, the Church, and unites us. The Holy Spirit does more: He commands that we "be filled" or "controlled" by His Spirit.

> **So roll up your sleeves, put your mind in gear, be totally ready to receive the gift that's coming when Jesus arrives. Don't lazily slip back into those old grooves of evil, doing just what you feel like doing. You didn't know any better than, you do now. As obedient children, let yourselves be pulled into a way of life shaped by God's life, a life energetic and blazing with holiness. God said, "I am holy; you be holy."**
>
> **(I Peter 1:13-16)**

We are not holy; it is the Holy Spirit Who conforms us to the image of Christ that makes us holy.

Three Types of Men

1. Unspiritual self (natural man)

Before you became a Christian the Bible refers to you as a "natural man" or the "unspiritual self."

> **The unspiritual self, just as it is by nature, can't receive the gifts of God's Spirit. There's no capacity for them. They seem like so much silliness.**
>
> **(I Corinthians 2:14)**

2. Christian (spiritually alive)

When you became a Christian you received the Lord Jesus Christ as your Savior simply by repentance and faith. It was at this time that Jesus Christ came into your life and the Holy Spirit renewed your spirit. The Bible refers to such an individual as "spiritually alive."

> **Spiritually alive, we have access to everything God's Spirit is doing.**
>
> **(I Corinthians 2:15)**

3. Carnal man (Christians acting like infants or selfishness)

The Apostle Paul refers to a third class of people:

> **But for right now, friends, I'm completely frustrated by your unspiritual dealings with each other and with God. You're acting like infants in relation to Christ, capable of nothing much more than nursing at the breast.**
>
> **(I Corinthians 3:1-2)**

These Christians were acting like infants, having their way own, fulfilling their own desires, and doing whatever pleased themselves. This was in opposition to being spiritually alive and controlled by the Holy Spirit.

Unspiritual Self   **Spiritually Alive**   **Self-Centered**

How can we be controlled by the Holy Spirit?

1. Cleansing—spiritual breathing

Obviously, the Holy Spirit cannot fill our lives if it is already full of sin and worthless things. Just as a person must repent of his sin and by faith receive Jesus Christ into his life as Savior and Lord, so must infant Christians practice spiritual breathing by *exhaling* (or turning from their sins) and *inhaling* (by inviting the Holy Spirit by faith to take control of their lives). We must all keep short accounts with God.

The basis of God's forgiveness is Christ's death on the cross, and when we confess our sins and agree with God that we have sinned, by faith we can accept God's forgiveness and we can be sure He forgives us.

> **If we admit our sins—make a clean breast of them—he won't let us down; he'll be true to himself. He'll forgive our sins and purge us of all wrongdoing.**
>
> **(I John 1:9)**

Here is an exercise to help us apply the principle of confession as a first step toward being controlled by the Holy Spirit. Take a piece of paper and write down all the unconfessed sin the Holy Spirit reveals in your life. Thank God for forgiveness and cleansing. Write across your list "I John 1:9." Now, destroy your list. Believe that God remembers your sin no more. The first step in being controlled by the Holy Spirit is cleansing.

> **. . . Christ made a single sacrifice for sins, and that was it! Then he sat down right beside God and waited for his enemies to cave in. It was a perfect sacrifice by a perfect person to perfect some very imperfect people.**

By that single offering, he did everything that needed to be done for everyone who takes part in the purifying process.

(Hebrews 10:12-14)

2. A renewing of your mind

The second step is a renewing of your mind, by understanding why you exist. Understanding the purpose of anything gives it meaning. God created us for His own glory. Our purpose must be to fulfill the reason God created us: to glorify Himself.

Do everything that way, heartily and freely to God's glory.

(I Corinthians 10:31)

The Christian should allow the Holy Spirit to control his mind so as not to become extreme but have balance and discernment. The Holy Spirit must be Lord of our minds. The goal of disciplined thinking is to produce in us greater likeness to and love for Christ.

If you've gotten anything at all out of following Christ, if his love has made any difference in your life, if being in a community of the Spirit means anything to you, if you have a heart, if you care—then do me a favor: Agree with each other, love each other, be deep-spirited friends. Don't push your way to the front; don't sweet-talk your way to the top. Put yourself aside, and help others get ahead. Don't be obsessed with getting your own advantage. Forget yourselves long enough to lend a helping hand. Think of yourselves the way Christ Jesus thought of himself.

(Philippians 2:1-5)

3. Allow the Holy Spirit to control your emotions.

The third step to be controlled by the Holy Spirit is to allow the Holy Spirit to control our emotions. We must see God's purpose in giving us the capacity for emotions. Our emotions are our "appreciators." God has given us emotions so we can appreciate God, His creation, and each other. We misuse our emotions when we cannot rise above hurt feelings, want sympathy more than solutions, and lose our poise and self-control.

Anger, frustration, hostility, and resentment are the misuse of our emotions. I have heard counselors say, "Oh, that is good. Don't keep pent-up emotions; get it out!" How many people do we know who sour their lives, who ruin all that is sweet and beautiful, who destroy their character, and even make bad blood. Calmness, serenity, compassion, enthusiasm, and warmth are the beautiful jewels of a rich emotional life. It is the result of a Spirit-controlled life. When the Holy Spirit controls our emotions, there will be stability.

> **Do you want to be counted wise, to build a reputation for wisdom? Here's what you do: Live well, live wisely, live humbly. It's the way you live, not the way you talk, that counts. Mean-spirited ambition isn't wisdom. Boasting that you are wise isn't wisdom. Twisting the truth to make yourselves sound wise isn't wisdom. It's the furthest thing from wisdom—it's animal cunning, devilish conniving. Whenever you're trying to look better than others or get the better of others, things fall apart and everyone ends up at the others' throats. Real wisdom, God's wisdom, begins with a holy life, and is characterized by getting along with others.**
>
> **(James 3:13-17)**

4. Allow the Holy Spirit to control your will.

The fourth step in being controlled by the Holy Spirit is to allow the Holy Spirit to control our will. When God is to take possession of us, it must be into the central will or personality that He enters. Here is a good rule to follow: if your heart is not right, your decisions will be wrong. Our biggest problem is not having the knowledge of God's will, but rather actually doing what God asks us to do. God always asks of us something we can do if we will.

God works from the inside out. Once the inner control of our will is in harmony with God's will, God will take care of the circumstances. We have a tendency to work from the outside. God asks us to do something and, if our heart is not right, we will make excuses. What God intends for us is not frustrated busyness but Spirit-directed fruitfulness. What God asks of us is just to cooperate with Him.

Those who trust God's action in them find that God's Spirit is in them—living and breathing God!

(Romans 8:5)

5. Accept the Holy Spirit's controlling of your whole person by faith.

The final step in being controlled by the Spirit is to accept The Holy Spirit's controlling of our person by faith. Allow God's Spirit to control every aspect of you. God wants the whole person. He wants to invade your spirit by the Holy Spirit and control your mind, emotions, and will. When the Holy Spirit is in control of your spirit and soul, your body will submit in obedience to do God's will. The following diagram will help you visualize the flow of the Holy Spirit through a properly ordered life.

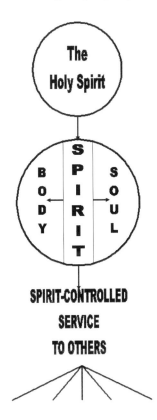

There are two good things that come from being controlled by the Holy Spirit:

1. It is the Holy Spirit Who is able to give us power for effective service.

> **When the Holy Spirit comes on you, you will be able to be my witnesses in Jerusalem, all over Judea and Samaria, even to the ends of the world.**

> **(Acts 1:8)**

2. The Holy Spirit makes it possible to live a holy life.

> **But what happens when we live God's way? He brings gifts into our lives, much the same way that fruit appears in an orchard—things like affection for others, exuberance about life, serenity. We develop a willingness to stick with things, a sense of compassion in the heart, and a conviction that a basic holiness permeates things and people. We find ourselves involved in loyal commitments, not needing to force our way in life, able to marshal and direct our energies wisely. Legalism is helpless in bringing this about; it only gets in the way. Among those who belong to Christ, everything connected with getting our own way and mindlessly responding to what everyone else calls necessities is killed off for good—crucified. Since this is the kind of life we have chosen, the life of the Spirit, let us make sure that we do not just hold it as an idea in our heads or a sentiment in our hearts, but work out its implications in every detail of our lives. That means we will not compare ourselves with each other as if one of us were better and another worse. We have far more interesting things to do with our lives. Each of us is an original.**

> **(Galatians 5:22-26)**

Where do all of these things come from? They are the Fruit of the Holy Spirit! They are produced by the Holy Spirit in our lives and they come from Him. The Fruit of the Spirit are character qualities that describe the Lord

Jesus Christ. The ministry of the Holy Spirit to the believer is to reproduce the life of Jesus Christ in us.

Everything comes from him;

Everything happens through him;

Everything ends up in him.

Always glory! Always praise!

Yes. Yes. Yes.

(Romans 11:36)

Let's summarize the steps in being controlled by the Holy Spirit.

1. Confess all known sin.
2. Have a renewing of your mind.
3. Allow the Holy Spirit to control your emotions.
4. Make all your decisions to please God.
5. By faith invite the Holy Spirit to take control of your whole person.

You may be wondering how to pray in faith to be controlled by the Holy Spirit. Pray in your own words, or you may wish to pray the following prayer: "Dear Father, I need you. I acknowledge that I have sinned against you. I thank you that you have forgiven my sins through Christ's death on the cross for me. I now invite The Holy Spirit to take control of the throne of my life. I pray this in the Name of Jesus Christ. As an expression of my faith, I now thank you for taking control of my entire life. Amen!"

In our next lesson we will see some of the character qualities God wants to develop in his disciples.

Application

Answer the following questions.

1. Who is the Holy Spirit?
   The Holy Spirit is _____ and He is a person.
2. All who believe in Jesus Christ as their Savior and Lord have _____ in them.
3. The Holy Spirit _____ us with Christ by helping us understand God's Word and joins with our spirit restoring our relationship with God; grants us God's mark of ownership; places us into the Body of Christ; and controls us to do the Will of God.
4. The Bible refers to someone who has never received Christ as Savior as an _____.
5. When you become a Christian, the Bible refers to you as _____.
6. When Christians become selfish, the Bible refers to them as _____.
7. _____ means exhaling or confessing our sins, and inhaling God's forgiveness.
8. Cleansing from sin, allowing the Holy Spirit to be Lord of our mind, submitting our emotions to the Holy Spirit, obeying God's Will; and yielding our whole personality to The Holy Spirit are steps in how to be _____ by the Holy Spirit.
9. List two good things that result from being controlled by the Holy Spirit. _____ and _____.

Assignment

Pray and ask God to take total control of you, right now!

CHAPTER SEVEN

FORGIVING SPIRIT:
Living a Transparent Life

God's intention for humanity is to glorify or please God the Father. When God created man He created him with a spirit in which the Holy Spirit would live and govern man's soul (intellect, emotions, and will.) Our spirit and soul would then use our body as the means of expression for God. It could be stated: "Humanity exists to express Deity."

Man, however, disobeyed God's instructions so God withdrew His Spirit from man's spirit. As a result, man became spiritually separated from God. He became self-centered instead of God-centered. It is not until man repents of his disobedience and by faith accepts God's gift of grace in the person of Jesus Christ that man is restored to a personal relationship with God. It is at this time that the Holy Spirit begins to develop character qualities in us and we become transparent so others can see Jesus Christ in us.

What are these character qualities that God wants to develop in us?

I. Humility

Humility can only be accomplished by *brokenness*. The soul must become the vessel for the Spirit's use. When we humble ourselves and rely on the Holy Spirit, we can learn God's Word with understanding, discern the spiritual condition of another, and share God's message with God's approval. Without the breaking of our soul, the Holy Spirit cannot be released to bless others.

Brokenness is the way of blessing and fruitfulness. It is the Spirit of God alone who gives life. When the Spirit is released, unbelievers may be born anew and believers may be established. Spiritual work is accomplished in God's coming out through our brokenness. *Brokenness* means that we, in humility, are willing to offer ourselves completely for God's use.

> **But all of you, leaders and followers alike, are to be down to earth with each other, for—God has had it with the proud, but takes delight in just plain people.**

> **(I Peter 5:5)**

Humility leads to forgiveness.

II. Forgiving Spirit

Another quality that God wants to develop in us is a forgiving spirit. In order to gain a clear conscience one must have a forgiving spirit. A clear conscience is listed in the Bible as one of the most essential weapons for successful spiritual growth. What is a clear conscience? A clear conscience is knowing that no one, God or man, can point a finger at you and say, "You've offended me, and you've never asked for my forgiveness."

> **Believe me, I do my best to keep a clear conscience before God and my neighbors in everything I do.**

> **(Acts 24:16)**

What can bring about a clear conscience and make a person free? Only the truth/reality can make a person free. If anyone relies on his own feelings and experiences, he will be defeated. Truth comes from the enlightenment from God. God's enlightenment brings about an inner radiance of a transparent life. God wants us to have a forgiving spirit and a clear conscience.

A clear conscience is necessary in order to *build genuine friendships.* The most basic quality needed for friendships is humility. When God makes it clear through His Word and the conviction of the Holy Spirit that you should go to the ones you have offended and ask for their forgiveness, they almost always become your best friends.

A clear conscience is necessary in *resolving conflicts in marriage.* When conflicts arise they are usually resolved when one member is willing to humble himself and ask for forgiveness.

One day Betty came for counseling.

Betty: "My husband and I used to attend church regularly, but things are different now. John refuses to go to church with me."

Counselor: "Betty, how important is it to you that John goes to church with you?"

Betty: "When we got married the church was the basis of our relationship and social life. Now, our relationship is deteriorating and our social life is nil."

Counselor: "Betty, I suggest that you make a list of everything you can think of that may have been an offense to John, and then go ask forgiveness for each item on your list."

Betty went home determined to carry this out. Two weeks later the Counselor received a note: "I did what you suggested and made amends with my husband. He was deeply touched. On Sunday we were in church together again."

A clear conscience is necessary in *overcoming temptation.* Satan uses a defiled conscience to defeat a Christian. The guilt of one's transgression becomes Satan's method of blackmail to go deeper and deeper into sin.

> If we claim that we experience a shared life with him and continue to stumble around in the dark, we're obviously lying through our teeth—we're not *living* what we claim. But if we walk in the light, God himself being the light, we also experience a shared life with one another, as the sacrificed blood of Jesus, God's Son, purges all our sin.
>
> (I John 1:6-7)

A clear conscience is necessary in *becoming an effective witness.*

> Be ready to speak up and tell anyone who asks why you're living the way you are, and always with the utmost courtesy. Keep a clear conscience before God so that when people throw mud at you, none of it will stick. They'll end up realizing that *they're* the ones who need a bath.
>
> (I Peter 3:15-16)

How to gain a clear conscience

a. List those whom you have offended and make a list of the offenses:

- Have you stolen items from anyone?
- Have you lied to anyone?
- Have you lost your temper with anyone?
- Have you damaged the reputation of anyone?
- Have you been ungrateful for what others have done for you?
- Have you held a bitter spirit toward anyone?

b. Ask those who have been offended for their forgiveness. Carefully choose the right wording.

Right wording: God has convicted me of how wrong I've been in (basic offense). I've called to ask, "Will you forgive me?"

Wrong wording: "**If** I've been wrong, please forgive me"; "I'm sorry"; "I was wrong but it wasn't all my fault."

c. Determine the proper method and time to ask forgiveness. The method may be a letter, phone call, or a personal visit. The time must be uninterrupted and convenient for the other person.

d. Be as brief and clear as possible and don't involve others in the confession.

e. Reflect sincere repentance.

Here are some special cautions when asking for forgiveness: If a sin is committed against God, then confession should be made to God alone. If a sin is committed against God and also another person, then confession should be made to God and the other person.

If a sin is committed against God and also a group, then confession should be made to both God and the group.

What do I do if the forgiveness is not granted by others? If you have repented and asked God and the offended person for forgiveness, then you have done your part. All that is expected of you is to pray for your friend.

III. Meekness

Meekness is a sign of humility. All who are broken by God are characterized by meekness. Every person has irritations. Meekness is responding to others as Christ would respond. Understanding the source, purpose, and how we should respond to these irritations is what develops character. Meekness starts when we begin to be more concerned about others than we are about ourselves. Jesus is our example. His whole life was a life of meekness. He humbled Himself, became as a servant, and even went to His death on the cross. All His disciples are to be like this. It is not a matter of a natural disposition. Meekness is something that is produced by the Holy Spirit. Meekness is not weakness. Meekness is compatible with great strength. A meek person is one who may so believe in standing for the truth that he will die for it, if necessary. Christian martyrs were meek, but they were never weak.

Meekness is not a matter of outward manner, but maturity of inward spirit. Meekness means that we allow the Holy Spirit to control our lips and mouth, and not say the things we feel like saying. We are to make sure we say only the things we believe the Holy Spirit would have us say. Meekness is essentially a true view of one's self in attitude and conduct with respect to others. A meek spirit goes a long way in solving irritations we cannot change.

Irritations come from different sources. Some irritations are irresolvable but extremely significant. God uses them to develop our inward qualities. If we respond to them with proper action, we allow God to achieve His purpose in us. Paul experienced a handicap and God explained the reason why He allowed such an irritation to Paul.

> **Because of the extravagance of those revelations, and so I wouldn't get a big head, I was given the gift of a handicap to keep me in constant touch with my limitations. Satan's angel did his best to get me down; what he in fact did was push me to my knees. No danger then of walking around high and mighty! At first I didn't think of it as a gift, and begged God to remove it. Three times I did that, and then he told me, My grace is enough; it's all you need. My strength comes into its own in your weakness.**

> **(2 Corinthian 12:7-8)**

Illnesses, defects, and personal handicaps which we are not able to change constitute sources of irritation. However, there are many irritations that we can change that are related to ourselves: bad habits, wrong attitudes, and incorrect decisions.

Our environment constitutes a source of irritation. Sometimes we can remove the source and at other times we cannot. Undesirable weather is not something we can control. Inconveniences of traffic may not be avoidable. However, snow and ice on the driveway can be removed. A dirty windshield can be cleaned.

People are the main source of our irritations. A neighbor who plays loud music or watches television late at night may keep us awake. A person with the idiosyncrasy of excessive talking can be annoying. A fellow worker who is inconsistent by giving praise when you are around, but has a critical attitude when you are not, can be very disturbing.

There are right and wrong responses to irritations. Whether irritations come from self, environment, or people, it is never proper to respond in anger, defending one's self, or blaming others. A Christian should respond as Christ would.

> **Be cheerful no matter what; pray all the time; thank God no matter what happens. This is the way God wants you who belong to Christ Jesus to live.**
>
> **(I Thessalonians 5:16-18)**

Christ's disciples are to minister to peoples' needs. Jesus always responded to others' true needs. He got at the root of their problem. We find it too easy to respond to people's symptoms. A parent yells at his child, and the child learns to yell back. A husband says things that hurt his wife, and the wife becomes angry. Ungodly behavior stems from spiritual deficiency. We must identify the possible cause of the irritation. Did I cause this by something I did or failed to do? If so, I must correct that which is wrong and ask forgiveness. It is only then that I can have the blessing of being used by God to minister to the person's spiritual need.

God allows irritations to come into our lives for the purpose of developing character qualities in us.

> **This is the kind of life you've been invited into, the kind of life Christ lived. He suffered everything that came his way so you would know that it could be done, and also know how to do it, step-by-step. He never did one thing wrong, Not once said anything amiss. They called him every name in the book and he said nothing back. He suffered in silence, content to let God set things right.**
>
> **(I Peter 2:21-23)**

Refusing to forgive results in anger and bitterness. Anger and bitterness carry physical, spiritual, emotional, and mental consequences. Physical consequences may be fatigue and loss of sleep. Spiritual consequences may be a lack of God's forgiveness toward us. Depression is one of the most significant emotional consequences of not forgiving people who wrong us. The moment we start hating a person, we mentally become that person's slave.

God desires to develop the character quality of meekness in us. Anger is the opposite of meekness. The meek will radiate inward beauty.

> Cultivate inner beauty, the gentle, gracious kind that God delights in.

> (I Peter 3:4)

IV. Joy

A transparent life knows how to handle irritations with a forgiving, meek spirit. A transparent life knows the joy in living for God and others instead of self living. What constitutes a transparent life? Transparent living allows the Holy Spirit to control one's life revealing the character qualities of Jesus Christ.

> To you who are ready for the truth, I say this: Love your enemies. Let them bring out the best in you, not the worst. When someone gives you a hard time, respond with the energies of prayer for that person. If someone slaps you in the face, stand there and take it. If someone grabs your shirt, gift wrap your best coat and make a present of it. If someone takes unfair advantage of you, use the occasion to practice the servant life. No more tit-for-tat stuff. Live generously.

> (Luke 6:27-30)

We benefit when we respond correctly to irritations. Your offenders will soon tell their friends of your godly response to them. Their response to you will give you many opportunities to share the Gospel and build new friendships. Lasting achievements in their lives will bring joy and fulfillment to you. As we permit God by His Spirit to express Himself through us in love, we experience joy that is an inward peace that is not affected by outward circumstances.

We rejoice because we have been delivered from our past sin. We rejoice because of the opportunities God has given to us in serving Him and others. We rejoice as we look forward to the Coming of Jesus Christ. Joy is the mark of maturity.

> I've told you these things for a purpose: that my joy might be your joy, and your joy wholly mature.

> (John 15:11)

Application

1. _____ can only be accomplished by brokenness.
2. _____ means that we in humility are willing to offer ourselves completely to God.
3. A _____ is knowing that no one, God or man, can point a finger at you and say "you've offended me and you've never asked for my forgiveness."
4. In asking for forgiveness you must reflect sincere _____
5. _____ is a sign of humility.
6. Meekness is something that is produced by the _____.
7. Three sources of irritations are:

   a) Personal handicaps
   b) _____
   c) _____

8. God allows irritations to come into our lives to develop _____.
9. _____ is the mark of maturity.

Assignment

Make arrangements to ask forgiveness from anyone whom the Holy Spirit brings to your mind as someone you have offended.

CHAPTER EIGHT

SERVANTHOOD: Serving God and Man

Only once in the Scriptures do we have Jesus announcing that He would provide an example for His disciples; then He washed their feet. When visitors would come in the house from the dusty streets, a servant would wash their feet. At the Last Supper they had all gathered but there was no one to wash their feet. The disciples wanted to know who was the greatest, but none of them wanted to wash the feet of the others. Jesus took a towel and a basin and washed their feet. This was a perfect example of greatness! Servanthood!

> Then he said, "Do you understand what I have done to you? You address me as 'Teacher' and 'Master,' and rightly so. That is what I am. So if I, the Master and Teacher, washed your feet, you must now wash each other's feet. I've laid down a pattern for you. What I've done, you do. I'm only pointing out the obvious. A servant is not ranked above his master; an employee doesn't give orders to the employer. If you understand what I'm telling you, act like it—and live a blessed life.

> (John 13:12-17)

Is it possible to perform acts of service without motives that are spiritual? Unless we surrender our rights and privileges and become dependent on the

Holy Spirit, our motives in service are unspiritual. Only as we become empty of self and dependent on God does the Holy Spirit use us. Self advertising does not grant us a place in the kingdom of God.

It is not a person's position or authority that makes him great, but the attitude of serving anyone in need. We are to be merciful and understanding with all who are weak and err, just as God's grace and mercy has been extended to each of us. Christian disciples are to reclaim the world's downtrodden people. We are commissioned to be loving, humble, obedient servants to everyone. Spiritual authority resides in a servant attitude.

> **That is what the Son of Man has done: He came to serve, not to be served—and then to give away his life in exchange for the many who are held hostage.**
>
> **(Matthew 20:28)**

We must follow Jesus' example and allow the Spirit of God to anoint us for ministry. Just as it cost Jesus His blood on Calvary to fulfill His role as Servant, so it will cost a Christian disciple nothing less than his life to find fulfillment as God's servant.

> **Remember, our Message is not about ourselves; we're proclaiming Jesus Christ, the Master. All we are is messengers, errand runners from Jesus for you. It started when God said, "Light up the darkness!" and our lives filled up with light as we saw and understood God in the face of Christ, all bright and beautiful . . . . We've been surrounded and battered by troubles, but we're not demoralized; we're not sure what to do, but we know that God knows what to do; we've been spiritually terrorized, but God hasn't left our side;**

Determining the Will of God

God's servants do not act on their own, do not depend on their self-confidence, nor seek personal reward. God's disciples have confidence in God, seek God's will in all decisions, and delight in obedience in doing the will of God. We do this through prayer.

We have confidence that, when we pray, God hears and answers our prayers.

> **And how bold and free we then become in his presence, freely asking according to his will, sure that he's listening. And if we're confident that he's listening, we know that what we've asked for is as good as ours.**

> **(1 John 5:14-15)**

In Lesson Five we learned that God answers prayer in different ways. Sometimes "Yes," at other times "No," and "Wait," when He knows we are not ready to receive the answer. We are not always spiritually mature enough to accept what God has in store for us at a particular time. We will discover that when God reveals His will for us, it will be a call to service. We must understand what true service is and by faith receive the answer joyfully, knowing God has His best in store for us.

What is True Service?

True service must be understood and practiced. True service is accomplished by the Holy Spirit in cooperation with our spirit. True service or discipline must be distinguished from legalism. "The action of a spiritual will in obedience to the Lord is called discipline. The action of the flesh in attempting obedience to God is called legalism."[15]

Legalism is service done by our human efforts.
> True service is dying to self.

Legalism exalts law above grace.
> True service is rendered out of obedience.

Legalism is the belief that one can earn one's way by service to God and to others.
> True service comes from a heart and life that is free.

Legalism binds God's people.
> True service welcomes all opportunities to serve.

Legalism discriminates concerning whom to serve.
> True service is content with God's approval.

Legalism chooses service that makes the most impression on others.
  True service serves because there is a need.
Legalism is affected by moods. It serves when there is a feeling to serve.
  True service is based on love and gratitude.
Legalism is based on external rewards.
  True service is accomplished in humility.
Legalism brings pride.
  True service is brought into our lives through learning humble service to others.

The more we serve others, the greater the development of compassion. We feel a new spirit of identification with people in pain. The more we serve others, the deeper love and joy we have in serving God. In *A Serious Call to a Devout and Holy Life*, William Law urged "that every day should be a day of humility by serving others." If we want humility, he counsels us to "condescend to all the weaknesses and infirmities of your fellow-creatures, cover their frailties, love their excellencies, encourage their virtues, relieve their wants, rejoice in their prosperities, compassionate their distress, receive their friendship, overlook their unkindness, forgive their malice, be a servant of servants, and condescend to do the lowest offices to the lowest of mankind."[16]

Ways to build a lifestyle of servanthood

There are many ways we can build a life-style of servanthood.

The gift of *Ministry* is serving in practical ways and may be a hidden ministry.

The gift of personal *Helpfulness* is a valuable gift of the Spirit. Every minister knows the value of his people who have the gift of helpfulness. These members help the work in a church go smoothly.

The gift of *Encouragement* relieves conflicts and builds meaningful relationships. We should not participate in speaking or listening to slanderous talk. Save your critical comments for yourself.

> **No insults, no fights. God's people should be bighearted and courteous.**
>
> **(Titus 3:2)**

The gift of *Hospitality* is a wonderful way to serve people. There is a great need today for people to open their homes to one another.

The gift of *Prayer*, bearing the burdens of each other and learning to listen is a great way to serve others. Just a little compassion will go a long way.

The gift of *Giving* as God prospers you is a beautiful way in contributing to meet the needs of others.

The gift of *Mercy* rendered in giving aid and care to the sick and needy brings healing and wholeness.

The gift of *Compassion* is a sweet gift to possess. Working with the disadvantaged is a great privilege.

> **Live creatively, friends. If someone falls into sin, forgivingly restore him, saving your critical comments for yourself. *You* might be needing forgiveness before the day's out. Stoop down and reach out to those who are oppressed. Share their burdens, and so complete Christ's law. If you think you are too good for that, you are badly deceived.**
>
> **(Galatians 6:1-3)**

Building a lifestyle of serverthood is the Holy Spirit prompting you to action. Those who expect recognition for their ministry never fully receive the joy that could have been theirs.

Who wants to live a wasted life?

Servanthood involves the lordship of Christ. It involves not only *recognizing* His lordship but *submitting* to His lordship. Servanthood is accomplished by commitment. Most Christians want to commit themselves to God. Who wants to live a wasted life? Servanthood means determining God's will for your life, and then becoming a servant to others as a way of living.

As people observe a Christian's life, they are to see the life of Jesus modeled before them. This is accomplished by the manifestation of :

The Fruit of the Holy Spirit

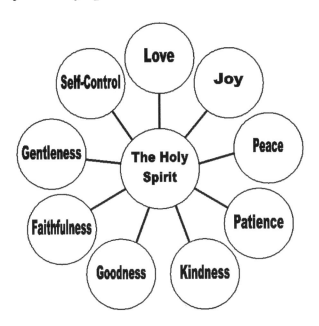

In the Book of Galatians the apostle Paul speaks of the Life of the Spirit. The "Fruit of the Spirit" consists of character qualities describing the very life of Jesus Christ. When Christ indwells us, our souls become as windows in which others can see the exalted life of Jesus Christ being lived out from us by the Holy Spirit.

> **Since this is the kind of life we have chosen, the life of the Spirit, let us make sure that we do not just hold it as an idea in our heads or a sentiment in our hearts, but work out its implications in every detail of our lives.**
>
> **(Galatians 5:25)**

Paul goes on to list the Fruit of the Spirit as

love,
joy,
peace,
long-suffering (patience),
gentleness (kindness),

goodness,
faith (faithfulness),
meekness (gentleness)
and self-control (temperance)

(Galatians 5:22-23 Authors revised list*)

These are the character traits that the Lord desires His servants to have. Since Jesus was indwelled by the same Holy Spirit who now indwells us, He produces the same good fruit in our lives that was manifested in His life.

Open Windows

How amazing it is that the God of all creation would design us to express Himself through us! It is as if God has made our lives to be as an open window for people to look in and see His lovely Son, Jesus Christ. In our homes at times we have blinds on our windows because we do not want others to see in. It is equally true of our souls. We can put blinds over our windows because we don't want others to see who we really are or what is going on. Blinds are the method we use to conceal the selfish life. We use blinds to hide the emptiness of our inner soul. When our blinds are closed, there is very little out-flowing of the Holy Spirit. God wants us to have open windows so the beautiful character of Christ may be seen.

Every quality mentioned in the list of the Fruit of the Holy Spirit is a facet of God's Divine Love. First Corinthians chapter 13 is often referred to as the "Love" chapter of the Bible.

LOVE—is the sum total of all of the fruit of the spirit.
JOY—"rejoices not in iniquity, but rejoices in the truth."
PEACE—"envies not"—peace with others and an inward peace.
LONGSUFFERING—"suffers long"—patience.
GENTLENESS—"bears all things."
GOODNESS—"thinks no evil, hopes all things."
FAITH—"believes all things."
MEEKNESS—"does not behave itself unseemly . . . is not easily provoked."
SELF-CONTROL—"endures all things"—temperance.

The work of the Holy Spirit within us is for life and living, enabling us to bear the fruit of the Holy Spirit and be a witness to the life we have in Jesus Christ. But God has provided for us even more.

The Gifts of the Holy Spirit

The work of the Holy Spirit upon man is for witness and service, causing us to manifest spiritual gifts. If a person has the proper life within and the outpouring of the Spirit without, he can be very useful to the Lord.

Fruit versus Gifts of the Spirit

A word of caution before we begin a discussion of the "Gifts" of the Spirit. Some people are more interested in the Gifts of the Spirit than the Fruit of the Spirit. Fruit is internal; gifts are an outward manifestation. It is true that the same Holy Spirit who bears His fruit in us also gives spiritual gifts to believers. However, one may possess gifts while being very spiritually immature. The Apostle Paul writes a letter to correct the situation in the first century church at Corinth. Some people in this church were exercising and misusing the Gifts of the Holy Spirit, while displaying very little Fruit of the Holy Spirit. We are not to be preoccupied with the gifts. Here is why! The Holy Spirit gives gifts as He wills. This is why we do not seek the gifts. The gifts are the property of the Holy Spirit. We don't own them. We don't even use them as we wish. We can't create or manufacture them. We don't grow them or produce them. They are the Holy Spirit's to give as He wills.

Everyone has natural gifts and talents. We were created in that way. It is good that we develop our natural gifts to their greatest potential. Never downplay your natural abilities. These natural abilities are not the gifts of the Spirit. Spiritual Gifts are the Holy Spirit's unique, divine gifts added to our natural abilities to accomplish God's Will.

Spiritual Gifts are given to those who are Christ's disciples. Every child of God receives God's Gifts at God's discretion. Not everyone receives the same gift or gifts, but everyone receives what God determines is necessary for each one to fulfill the ministry that God has called him to accomplish.

> **Each of us finds our meaning and function as a part of his body. But as a chopped-off finger or cutoff toe we wouldn't amount to much, would we? So since we find ourselves fashioned into all these excellently formed and marvelously functioning parts in Christ's body, let's just go ahead and be what we were made to be, without enviously or pridefully comparing ourselves with each other, or trying to be something we aren't. If you preach, just preach God's Message, nothing else; if you help, just help, don't take over; if you teach, stick to your teaching; if you give encouraging guidance, be careful that you don't get bossy; if you're put in charge, don't manipulate; if you're called to give aid to people in distress, keep your eyes open and be quick to respond; if you work with the disadvantaged, don't let yourself get irritated with them or depressed by them. Keep a smile on your face.**
>
> **(Romans 12:5-8)**

Paul lists these Spiritual Gifts:

Prophecy—speaking out the truth.
Ministry—serving in practical ways.
Teaching—explaining the Word of God and applying it to people's lives.

Exhortation—speaking words of encouragement to others.
Giving—contributing to meet others' needs.
Leadership—the ability to administer, govern, rule, and be a servant to all.
Mercy—giving aid to the sick and needy.

Another list of gifts can be found in I Corinthians chapter 12. This set of gifts is unique to particular situations and times. As the church gathers, different gifts may be exercised depending on the needs of the people in that church and at that time. These gifts are given so that the Body of Christ functions in unity. The Holy Spirit speaks and works through this one, and that one, and another one at His discretion.

> **Each person is given something to do that shows
> who God is: Everyone gets in on it, everyone
> benefits. All kinds of things are handed out by the
> Spirit, and to all kinds of people! The variety is
> wonderful:**
> **wise counsel**
> **clear understanding**
> **simple trust**
> **healing the sick**
> **miraculous acts**
> **proclamation**
> **distinguishing between spirits**
> **tongues**
> **interpretation of tongues.**
>
> **All these gifts have a common origin, but are handed out
> one by one by the one Spirit of God. He decides who gets what,
> and when.**
>
> **(I Corinthians 12:5-11)**

The third list of Gifts is found in Ephesians chapter 4. Here are four Gifts that are given to the church as a whole.

Apostles—leaders of new ministries of outreach.
Prophets—those who tell the truth and the consequences of not
    following God's will.

Evangelists—those who share the Good News, the gospel of Jesus Christ as a way of life.

Pastors/Teachers—those who teach believers, equipping them for service.

> **He handed out gifts of apostle, prophet, evangelist, and pastor-teacher to train Christ's followers in skilled servant work, working within Christ's body, the church.**
>
> **(Ephesians 4:11)**

How do all these gifts fit together? God knows who you are. He knows who He created you to be and which gifts, talents, and abilities He put into your life. God knows how to place us within a body of people to accomplish His ministry. Spiritual gifts are to be exercised for the building up of the church. God's rule of action is that each believer is to be a servant to all.

What are my Spiritual Gift/Gifts?

Each of us will have one or more of these gifts. Let's stop for a moment and ask ourselves, "Which spiritual gift/gifts do I have?"

God has called us to be His servants. He has gifted us to do the work of serving. He has placed within us the Holy Spirit to conform us into the image of His Son, Jesus Christ. He is the servant to all and the servant of all. We are to follow His example.

Application

1. It is not a person's position that makes him great, but the _____ of _____ anyone in _____.
2. It will cost a Christian disciple nothing less than his _____ to find fulfillment as God's servant.
3. The fruit of the Spirit consists of _____ qualities describing the life of Christ.
4. _____ is the belief that one can earn one's way by service to God and to others.
5. True service is based on _____ and gratitude.
6. _____ are methods we use that reveal the selfish life.
7. God wants us to have open _____ so the character of Christ is seen.
8. Every quality in the list of the Fruit of the Spirit is a facet of divine _____.
9. If a person has the proper life within and the outpouring of the Spirit without, he can be very _____ for the Lord.
10. A person may possess spiritual _____ while being Spiritually immature.
11. Every child of God receives spiritual gifts at _____ direction.
12. Spiritual gifts are to be exercised for the building up of the _____.

Assignment

Make a list of the ministries you have done this week.

CHAPTER NINE

THE DIVINE WAY OF LIFE:
Living a Life of Giving

To be a servant of the Most High requires daily obedience. It never happens automatically. It is a conscious decision of making Jesus Lord.

> **"Why are you so polite with me, always saying 'Yes, sir',
> and 'that's right, sir', but never doing a thing I tell you?"**

> **(Luke 6:46)**

The Lordship of Christ

Jesus is Lord! He is the owner and master of all creation. Our belief or lack of belief can never change the fact of His lordship. Jesus Christ is Lord! Ultimately, everyone will acknowledge Jesus as Lord, willingly or unwillingly.

> **Because of that obedience, God lifted him high and
> honored him far beyond anyone or anything, ever, so that
> all created beings in heaven and on earth—even those long
> ago dead and buried—will bow in worship before this Jesus
> Christ, and call out in praise that he is the Master of all, to
> the glorious honor of God the Father.**

> **(Philippians 2:9-11)**

Acknowledging Jesus as Lord means that I have confessed with my mouth and believed in my heart that Jesus Christ is the Gift of eternal life. We are to continually commit our mind, emotions, and will to the lordship of Jesus Christ. Everything in your life must be subject to Jesus' lordship. God cares about everything in your life. As a Christian disciple, you have died with Christ and your life belongs to Him.

> **So, chosen by God for this new life of love, dress in the wardrobe God picked out for you: compassion, kindness, humility, quiet strength, discipline. Be even-tempered, content with second place, quick to forgive an offense. Forgive as quickly and completely as the Master forgave you. And regardless of what else you put on, wear love. It's your basic, all—purpose garment. Never be without it.**

> **(Colossians 3:12-14)**

Since Jesus is Lord, you should desire to please Him in everything. God will grant you His guidance when you ask sincerely. The Bible promises that those who truly seek to please Him will get the direction they need from Him.

> **Don't bargain with God. Be direct. Ask for what you need. This isn't a cat-and-mouse, hide-and-seek game we're in.**

> **(Matthew 7:7)**

Jesus said:

> **"Anyone who intends to come with me has to let me lead. You're not in the driver's seat; _I_ am. Don't run from suffering; embrace it. Follow me and I'll show you how. Self-help is no help at all. Self-sacrifice is the way, my way, to saving yourself, your true self. What good would it do to get everything you want and lose you, the real you? What could you ever trade your soul for?"**

> **(Mark 8:34-37)**

In the above words of Jesus it becomes evident that any self-help effort will produce failure, because God's divine way of living is produced only by God's Spirit, and is a life of giving.

How can we experience a life of giving?

God's answer to man's need is a Person. It is the Person of Jesus Christ who becomes a divine way of life in us.

> **Everything that we have—right thinking and right living, a clean slate and a fresh start—comes from God by way of Jesus Christ. That's why we have the saying, "If you're going to blow a horn, blow a trumpet for God."**
>
> **(I Corinthians 1:30-31)**

Jesus Christ set us free from our sin so we could belong to Him. He paid the price. He separated us from sin for Himself. Through Him we come into complete harmony and a right standing with Him. We need to be taken up with Jesus Christ as Lord. Our Heavenly Father desires to have His Son express His life in and through us.

This new life in Christ with God is accomplished by the *cross*. What is the meaning and purpose of the cross? We can understand its meaning more fully if we see the cross in its three dimensions.

The Cross demonstrated by God the Father

When God created the universe, He gave of Himself in that creative act. When God created man, He breathed into his nostrils the breath of life. He gave of His own Life when He created man in His own image. This life of *giving* has always been expressed in the Godhead. The cross as a life of *giving* is in contrast to a life of *getting*.

God created the first man and woman with free moral choice. The purpose was so that they could *give* themselves back to God. In turn, this would show they truly loved their Father and desired to serve Him. In the Garden of Eden God asked Adam to live a life of *giving* by becoming a father himself (populating the world after his kind) and, as a father, ruling over it. If Adam would choose God's way and obey by *giving* himself to God's plan, he would live a life of selfless giving rather than selfish living. We all know what happened. Adam chose his own way and he became sinful and separated from God.

The Cross exemplified by the Son at Calvary

Calvary is the historical place where Jesus died on the cross. The cross became necessary only because man chose to go his own way rather than God's way. If all you know about the cross is that there was one 2000 years ago, then you have missed the point of the cross.

The Father sent His Son, Jesus Christ, to walk among us and once again demonstrate a life of *giving*. Jesus was led by the Holy Spirit into the wilderness. It was here He met Satan. Jesus would do nothing for Himself. He refused to turn stones into bread to satisfy His physical hunger. He would not cast Himself down from the temple and use His power to save Himself. He would not bow down and worship Satan, even for one moment, in order to rule over all the kingdoms on earth. They were already His anyway. He was committed to one thing: to live a life of *giving* by doing the Will of the Father.

**The test was over. The Devil left. And in his place, angels!
Angels came and took care of Jesus' needs.**

(Matthew 4:11)

A life of *getting* is unacceptable to God the Father. A life of *giving* is God's way and plan. Even the religious leaders of Jesus' day would not accept Jesus and His way of living because it exposed their selfish lives. So they put Him on a cross at Calvary, which revealed their hatred. Whenever love and hate meet each other, a cross will be formed. So the cross demonstrated by the Father was exemplified by the Son at Calvary.

The Cross as a way of life modeled by the Christian

We must not interpret the cross as merely a remedy for man's sin. The cross must be modeled as a way of life of *Giving*. The cross must become a power in our lives, as we *give* ourselves to God and in loving service to each other. The cross in the life of the believer means, "I serve God in God's way."

Today many people want to serve God if they can do it their way, with the right person of their choosing, and in the place of their choosing. It is not that people don't want to serve God, but they want to serve God if it is doing just what *they* want to do, and in the way *they* want it done, and if it doesn't interfere in any way with *their* plans. The result is that many of God's people are living barren, empty lives and missing God's blessings.[17]

Here is another way to understand the meaning of the cross.

> **"Listen carefully: Unless a grain of wheat is buried in the ground, dead to the world, it is never any more than a grain of wheat. But if it is buried, it sprouts and reproduces itself many times over. In the same way, anyone who holds on to life just as it is destroys that life. But if you let it go, reckless in your love, you'll have it forever, real and eternal. If any of you wants to serve me, then follow me. Then you'll be where I am, ready to serve at a moments' notice. The Father will honor and reward anyone who serves me."**
>
> **(John 12:24-26)**

Any farmer plants good seed, seed with life in it. Seed is planted for reproduction. We are as seed in God's hand. When we are willing to serve God in God's way, we will serve in His power and the fruit will be for His glory.

The concept of self-fulfillment is comfortable for us. But the concept of the cross reminds us that the divine way of living is a life of self-denial and self-sacrifice. The self-fulfillment Jesus is talking about is vastly different from humanistic self-fulfillment. Self-denial means the interests of others become more important to us than our own interests.

Submitting to God's ways is laying down the burden of getting our own way. Selfish attitudes are put to death because of the cross and this grants to us the freedom to see other people through the eyes of the Holy Spirit. In submission we become free to value other people. Jesus—others—self is the proper order of importance and gives us the ability to love others unconditionally. A life of giving is the life of freely accepting God's divine way of living.

Experiencing Resurrection Power

The cross has two sides but they are inseparable. On one side is death; on the other side is resurrection. On the death side, we recognize our sinful nature and account it to be dead. On the life side, the resurrected life, we find it consists of three aspects:

(1) to be alive with the Lord
(2) to have the Lord living in me
(3) to be living for the Lord.

It is upon reaching this resurrected stage that we experience the resurrected power for service and victory.

> **Our old way of life was nailed to the cross with Christ, a decisive end to that sin-miserable life—no longer at sin's every beck and call! What we believe is this: If we get included in Christ's sin-conquering death, we also get included in his life-saving resurrection.**
>
> **(Romans 6:6-7)**

The moment we invite Jesus Christ to come into our life, the Holy Spirit indwells us, exalting Jesus Christ as our Lord.

Our self-denial and Christ's resurrected power in us prepares us for the practical outflow for service. Richard Foster, in *Celebration of Discipline*, mentions seven areas of submission in following the cross-life as a divine way of living.

1. Submission to the Triune God—at the beginning of each day we submit our body, mind, and spirit into the hands of God.
2. Submission to the Word of God—We submit ourselves to hear, receive and obey the Word of God.
3. Submission to our family—Members of our family make allowances for each other.

4. Submission to those we meet in the course of our daily lives. We perform acts of kindness.
5. Submission to the believing community. If there are tasks to be accomplished, we consider them carefully.
6. Submission to the broken and despised—widows, orphans, the undefended, the downtrodden, and the rejected.
7. Submission to the world. Environmental responsibilities and starving people.[18]

Jesus the Lord demands that His disciples adopt the divine way of living. The cross illustrates for us that it is a life of self-denial and submission to do the Father's will. This divine way of life results in His resurrection power and fruitfulness. The cost of this commitment is nothing less than your total self.

Application

1. _____ will acknowledge Jesus Christ as Lord willingly or unwillingly.
2. Acknowledging Jesus Christ as Lord means that I have _____ with my mouth and _____ in my heart that Jesus Christ is the Gift of eternal Life.
3. The Bible promises that those who truly seek Him will get the _____ they need from Him.
4. The divine way of living is produced only by _____ and is a life of giving.
5. Our Heavenly Father desires to have His sons _____ His life in and through us.
6. This new life of God in Christ is accomplished by the _____.
7. This life of _____ is God's way and plan.
8. In submission we become free to _____ other people. Jesus, others, and self is the proper order.
9. Our self denial and Christ's _____ power in us prepares us for the practical outflow for service.
10. The divine way of life results in His resurrection power and our _____.

Assignment

Find someone this week in need and provide that need for them even at a sacrifice to yourself.

CHAPTER TEN

SPIRITUAL WARFARE:
Putting on Spiritual Armament for Battle

New Christians are normally vague about spiritual warfare and lack a clear insight as to the schemes, assaults, temptations, and counterfeits of the Devil. When we become burdened and oppressed with issues of life, determining the source of the difficulties leads us to proper solutions.

Do these difficulties come from:

1. God
2. Natural factors
3. The enemy of God, Satan

Is Adversity Ever Caused by God?

Difficulties that come from God come in the form of discipline. We call it "chastisement." Chastisement is an act of God used as His method for building character.

> So don't feel sorry for yourselves. Or have you forgotten how good parents treat children, and that God regards you as *his* children? My dear child, don't shrug off God's discipline, but don't be crushed by it either. It's the child he loves that he disciplines; the child he embraces, he also corrects.

> **(Hebrews 12:5)**

When a child of God willfully disobeys the will of God, chastisement can be expected. God, as our heavenly Father, has the wisdom and right to apply the rod as concerns our eternal welfare.

Why did this happen?

Other difficulties come as the result of the violation of natural laws of cause and effect. We refer to these as "reapings." We would be amazed to realize how much illness comes to us in retribution for foolish judgments in the light of natural law. Nature brings its own chastisement. If we consider ourselves no more than a garbage can, and put all the garbage into it, then we will become physical junk. If you stay out in the sun too long, you will become sunburned. The natural law takes its effect on you. If you refuse to eat, sleep, and exercise properly, you likely will become ill. The illness is not from God, nor from God's enemy, but from the violation of natural law.

Who Is Responsible for This?

"Hindrances" can occur when we determine to do God's will and fulfill God's purposes. Satan and his forces will oppose you; oppression will set in, and depression can overcome you. Satan is the source and he is the hinderer and his methods are legion.

> **I, Paul, tried over and over to get back, but Satan stymied us each time.**
>
> **(I Thessalonians 2:18)**

Evil spirits are at work today, inside as well as outside the church. They attack and deceive every human being wherever they can find conditions fulfilled to enable them to manifest their power. Deceiving spirits desire to be your foe or hinderer, do evil, create hate, be unjust, tell lies, keep you ignorant, keep you in the dark, and keep you from the truth.

The subject of spiritual warfare is often ignored by many Christians. This subject is extremely important if we are to live victoriously over our enemies. We need to have some understanding of good angels, bad angels, and the armor God has given us to fight our enemies.

How do good angels help us defeat our enemies?

"Angels are created, spiritual beings with moral judgment and high intelligence, but without physical bodies."[19]

> **We look at this Son and see the God who cannot be seen. We look at this Son and see God's original purpose in everything created. For everything, absolutely everything, above and below, visible and invisible, rank after rank after rank of angels—*everything* got started in him and finds its purpose in him.**
>
> (Colossians1:15-16)

God has given us angels to guard and protect us. The power of angels is used to battle against the evil demonic powers under the control of Satan. When we are delivered from a danger or distress, we might suspect that angels have been sent by God to help us, and we should be thankful.

> **Isn't it obvious that all angels are sent to help out with those lined up to receive salvation?**
>
> (Hebrews 1:14)

Angels join with us in worshiping God. Though Scripture does not give us a figure for the number of angels God created, it is a very great number. When we come to worship, we come into the presence of innumerable angels. What a difference this should make in our worship services, just knowing many angels are present worshipping with us.

> **The invisible Jerusalem is populated by throngs of festive angels and Christian citizens.**
>
> (Hebrews 12:22)

In 1816 James Montgomery wrote a beautiful hymn that we sing during the Christmas Season: "Angels From the Realms of Glory."

Angels, from the realms of glory, wing your flight o'er all the earth; Ye who sang creation's story now proclaim Messiah's birth: Come and worship, come and worship, worship Christ, the newborn King.

Does not Scripture promise

For he will give his angels charge of you to guard you in all your ways.

(Psalm 91:11 RSV)

How do Satan and his demons prevent us from doing God's Will?

The previous section of this lesson leads naturally to a consideration of Satan and demons. The term "Satan" means "adversary." In our culture many have taken their beliefs about Satan from a Halloween party. He is depicted as wearing a red suit, having horns and a tail, and carrying a pitchfork. They think of Satan as a superstition along with goblins and ghosts.

The Biblical view of Satan is that he appears as "an angel of light." Satan and demons were good angels who were created, spiritual beings with moral judgment and high intelligence, who sinned against God and who now continually work evil in the world.

Something happened in Heaven that caused the fall of Satan and his demons. Isaiah fourteen may be a reference to the fall of Satan. Isaiah is describing the judgment of God on the king of Babylon. However, you come to a section with strong language that seems to fit the fall of Satan.

"How you are fallen from heaven, O Day Star, son of Dawn! How you are cut down to the ground, you who laid the nations low! You said in your heart, 'I will ascend to heaven; above the stars of God I will set my throne on high; I will sit on the mount of assembly in the far north; I will ascend above the heights of the clouds, I will make myself like the Most High.' But you are brought down to Sheol, to the depths of the Pit.

(Isaiah 14:12-15 RSV)

If this is referring to Satan's fall, the sin of Satan is described as one of pride and attempting to be equal to God. The Bible uses several names for Satan. He is called the Devil, the serpent, Beelzebub, the ruler of this world, the prince of the power of the air, and the evil one.

Satan is a created being. He is not like God in that he does not know all things, and he can only be present at one place at a time. When Satan rebelled against God, other angelic spirits followed him and they were cast out of heaven. These other angelic spirits are called "demons." Demons are under the direction of Satan and he has organized them to war against the will of God, against God's purposes in the world, and against all Christians.

Methods Satan Uses to Attack Christians

1. *Temptation.* Satan has an arsenal of attacks he has given his demonic army to use against God's people. Demons will try to use temptations. Satan and his workers try to get us to disobey God's Word. Temptation of itself is not sin, but *following* the temptation to its conclusion results in sin. When we sin against God, guilt develops.

   > **No test or temptation that comes your way is beyond the course of what others have had to face. All you need to remember is that God will never let you down; he'll never let you be pushed past your limit; he'll always be there to help you come through it.**
   >
   > **(I Corinthians 10:13)**

2. *Deception.* Deception opens our minds to doubting God's Word, distorts the truth, allows false religion, false doctrine, and blinds our minds from the truth.
3. *Illness.* Not all physical sickness is from Satan, but physical and psychological illnesses of various types may result from fear, confusion, envy, pride, jealousy, and impurity, which come from Satan and demonic activities.
4. *Accusations.* Slander, unjust criticism, lies, murder, persecution, ridicule, and accusations—all are of Satan. Satan constantly accuses us before God.

> **The Accuser of our brothers and sisters thrown out, who accused them day and night before God.**

> **(Revelation 12:10)**

5. *Discouragement.* Satan and his forces cause discouragement, feelings of worthlessness, and even despair which can result in suicide. Satan and demons are behind the evil in the world.

God has provided His armor for us to protect us against Satan

God knew the outward protection of good angels would not be sufficient against the power of evil in the world. So, in addition, He provided for us inward armor so we could defeat the enemy. There is victory over Satan's attacks. The Apostle Paul uses a description drawn from equipment worn and used by the Roman soldier to introduce us to the equipment God wears and provides for us in the battle against our enemies.

What is the key to overcoming Satan's forces? Paul gives us the answer in Ephesians 6:10-20.

> **God is strong, and he wants you strong. So take everything the Master has set out for you, well-made weapons of the best materials. And put them to use so you will be able to stand up to everything the Devil throws your way. This is no afternoon athletic contest that we'll walk away from and forget about in a couple of hours. This is for keeps, a life-or-death fight to the finish against the Devil and all his angels. Be prepared. You're up against far more than you can handle on your own. Take all the help you can get, every weapon God has issued, so that when it's all over but the shouting you'll still be on your feet. Truth, righteousness, peace, faith and salvation are more than words. Learn how to apply them. You'll need them throughout your life. God's Word is an *indispensable* weapon. In the same way, prayer is essential in this ongoing warfare. Pray hard and long. Pray for your brothers and sisters. Keep your eyes open. Keep each other's spirits up so that no one falls behind or drops out . . . . Love mixed with faith be yours from God the Father and from the Master, Jesus Christ. Pure**

grace and nothing but grace be with all who love our Master, Jesus Christ.

(Ephesians 6:10-18, 23-24)

In the light of the seriousness of this warfare, the Christian cannot be self-reliant. We must continuously depend upon God. Without His help we would never make it. To be successful in this battle we must put on all the armor God has provided for us. The conflict is serious because the battle is not against natural forces, but spiritual: principalities, powers, rulers, and spiritual wickedness. The enemies are real, but, thank God, they can be overcome by His grace.

Let's examine each piece of the armor God provides.

1. The Belt of Truth

Truth is light, and Jesus is the Truth. Walk in truth before God and men, and you will not be defeated by deception. A person of integrity, with a clear conscience, can face the enemy without fear. A person who operates in the realm of the truth of God's Word will not be defeated in battle.

2. The Breastplate of Righteousness

The breastplate of a Roman soldier was usually composed of metallic scales, but sometimes it was made of leather or bronze. It covered the torso and protected the vital organs of the body: the heart, the lungs, etc. It saved the soldier from becoming mortally wounded. Similarly, the person who is just or righteous, because he has accepted Christ's righteousness, will not be mortally wounded in the spiritual warfare in which he is engaged. The fruit of righteousness is related to conduct. Satan is an accuser, but if we live a godly life in the power of the Holy Spirit, his accusations will be found false.

3. The Shoes of the Gospel of Peace

The soldier needed sure footing to enable him to march and move quickly. The sole of the military shoe was studded with nails to permit surefootedness. The gospel of peace is a fitting way of stating that a Christian must be prepared with the gospel which has peace as its message. We must be at peace with God and at peace with each other if we are to defeat the Devil. As God's ambassadors of peace we take this gospel of peace wherever we go.

4. The Shield of Faith

Believers should never be without the shield of faith. The shield was constructed of layers of bronze and oxhide, and usually about four feet high and two feet long. The shield protected the soldier from the arrows and fiery darts that had been dipped in pitch and set afire. The shield would cause the arrows to fall to the ground harmlessly. "The edges of these shields were so constructed that an entire line of soldiers could interlock shields and march into the enemy like a solid wall."[20] Just as a soldier could not afford to be without this protective shield at any time, so we as followers of Christ cannot afford to be without faith. Our faithfulness grants us the ability to trust the Lord in all situations. Satan shoots fiery darts at our minds attempting to cause us to disobey God. The shield of faith and faithfulness gives us the victory over all these fiery darts.

5. The Helmet of Salvation

The helmet was made of bronze with leather attachments. It protected a soldier's head. "The head" refers to a person's will, an important part of his intellectual process that gives him hope and assurance of salvation. The head also symbolizes the mind which needs protection from the fiery darts of thoughts that are lies and are hateful. The head also symbolizes our emotions which need protection from their misuse by being unkind and unloving.

6. The Sword of the Spirit

The sword was a piercing or cutting weapon with which a soldier might stab or slash the enemy. The Sword of the Spirit is the Word of God. This is our **offensive** weapon. God's Word is Truth! Satan flees when God's soldiers obey the truth. Satan trembles at God's Word. The Word of God pierces the heart, while a physical sword can only pierce the body.

7. Prayer

Prayer and watchfulness are needed in this conflict. Prayer must be in the Spirit in order to be effective. We are always to be in an attitude of prayer or having a consistent prayer life. If Christians practice prayer as a way of life, when the special times of need come, they will be prepared for them.

8. Love

Love is the super weapon of the Christian. Our love is to be directed toward God with all our heart, soul, and strength. This love is also to be directed toward others. Love is something we **do**. It must be demonstrated in speech and deed. The Holy Spirit stands ready to pour love into our hearts. Love is the fruit of His Spirit. Love never fails. Love conquers all. There is no situation, no problem, no difficulty, which cannot be conquered by love. Love is the greatest of all the gifts!

This conflict is a real one; the enemies are spiritual forces that are not limited to the physical realm. But God has provided sufficient necessary equipment for us to be victorious in this battle.

> **Keep a cool head. Stay alert. The Devil is poised to pounce, and would like nothing better than to catch you napping. Keep your guard up. You're not the only ones plunged into these hard times.**

> **(I Peter 5:8)**

Jesus Christ defeated Satan at the cross, and through Him we have victory over Satan. We must give thanks to Jesus for having won the victory over Satan. We are to submit to Jesus Christ and resist Satan, then Satan will flee from us. As a child of God, Jesus lives in you through his Holy Spirit. He is more powerful than Satan.

> **He stripped all the spiritual tyrants in the universe of their sham authority at the Cross and marched them naked through the streets.**

> **(Colossians 2:15)**

God has already achieved victory over Satan and all evil powers by Christ's resurrection and exaltation. In the lives of Christians our emphasis is not to be on the influence of evil activities, but we are to learn how to grow and do the will of God : Making Disciples!

APPLICATION

1. Difficulties that come from God come in the form of _____.
2. _____ is an act of God used as God's Method for building character.
3. _____ occur when we violate natural law.
4. Satan is the source of _____.
5. How do good angels help us defeat our enemies?
   _____.
6. The term _____ means adversary.
7. Evil angelic spirits are called _____.
8. List five methods Satan uses to attack the Christian.

   a) _____
   b) _____
   c) _____
   d) _____
   e) _____

9. List the eight pieces of spiritual armor God has provided for us.

   1. _____ 2. _____ 3. _____
   4. _____ 5. _____ 6. _____
   7. _____ 8. _____.

10. _____ is the greatest of all the gifts.

Assignment

As you begin each day through prayer put on all the armor of God.

CHAPTER ELEVEN

THE CHURCH:
My Participation in the Local Church

In its true spiritual reality, the church is the fellowship of all genuine believers. The church in this sense is invisible. The invisible church is the church as God sees it. There are several expressions in the Bible that are used to describe the church:

- ❖ the body of Christ
- ❖ the people of God
- ❖ the elect
- ❖ the communion of saints
- ❖ the company of the redeemed
- ❖ the bride of Christ
- ❖ the family of God

All people who have put their trust in Jesus Christ alone for their salvation receive God's grace and are placed into His invisible body called the church. They automatically become members of the family of God. The members of the family of God are united by one Lord, one faith, and one baptism. The church is *catholic*, which means *universal*. The family of God includes people from all nations.

The church becomes visible in the gathering of Christians in local areas for corporate worship, fellowship, prayer, and to be active witnesses in the mission of the church. The church is also called the body of Christ. The body of Christ functions in unity. Our physical body is made up of living parts. The body functions in unity by each part contributing to and being dependent on the other parts. Our physical body displays unity and diversity. Each part has its own function. In a similar way each member in the family of God has been gifted by God to contribute to the work of the whole body.

> **All these gifts have a common origin, but are handed out one by one by the one Spirit of God. He decides who gets what, and when. You can easily enough see how this kind of thing works by looking no further than your own body. Your body has many parts—limbs, organs, cells—but no matter how many parts you can name, you're still one body. It's exactly the same with Christ. By means of his one Spirit, we all said good-bye to our partial and piecemeal lives. We each used to independently call our own shots, but then we entered into a large and integrated life in which *he* has the final say in everything. (This is what we proclaimed in word and action when we were baptized.) Each of us is now a**

part of his resurrection body, refreshed and sustained at one fountain—his Spirit—where we all come to drink.

(I Corinthians 12:12-13)

Participating in the local church involves eight elements: corporate worship, corporate prayer, receiving the sacraments, fellowship, stewardship, service, Bible study, and disciple-making.

Corporate Worship

To worship is to know, to feel, and to experience the resurrected Christ when we gather as the people of God. God actively seeks worshipers.

> **"It's who you are and the way you live that count before God. Your worship must engage your spirit in the pursuit of truth. That's the kind of people the Father is out looking for: those who are simply and honestly *themselves* before him in their worship. God is sheer being itself—Spirit. Those who worship him must do it out of their very being, their spirits, their true selves, in adoration."**

(John 4:23-24)

Forms and rituals do not produce worship, nor does the disuse of them. We can have the best liturgy, techniques, and methods but we have not worshiped the Lord until God's Spirit touches our spirit. The New Testament does not prescribe a particular form for worship. We are free in Christ to use whatever forms will enhance our worship. Forms are not to be used for entertainment only in worship, but to lead us into true worship.

When Jesus was tempted by the Devil in the wilderness, the Devil offered Jesus all the kingdoms on earth, if Jesus would worship him. Jesus points out the object of our worship.

> **"Worship the Lord your God, and only him. Serve him with absolute single-heartedness."**
>
> **(Matthew 4:10)**

We are to praise God for Who He is, and thank Him for all He has done. The most important commandment of Jesus is:

> **The Lord your God is one; so love the Lord God with all your passion and prayer and intelligence and energy.**
>
> **(Mark 12:30)**

When we, the body of Christ, come into public worship, we should come with anticipation, expecting to hear from God. Spirit-inspired preaching breathes life into worship. Heart-preaching inflames the spirit of worship. There is nothing more deadening than head-preaching that is humanly inspired.

> **Let the Word of Christ—the Message—have the run of the house. Give it plenty of room in your lives. Instruct and direct one another using good common sense. And sing, sing your hearts out to God! Let every detail in your lives—words, actions, whatever—be done in the name of the Master, Jesus, thanking God the Father every step of the way.**
>
> **(Colossians 3:16-17)**

Corporate Prayer

In Chapter Five we discussed one's personal prayer life. The Scriptures, however, also call us to corporate prayer as we assemble together.

> **That day about three thousand took him at his word, were baptized and were signed up. They committed themselves to the teaching of the apostles, the life together, the common meal, and the prayers.**
>
> **(Acts 2:42)**

Throughout the New Testament there is a strong emphasis on corporate praying. The Christians were deeply involved in one another's lives, praying for one another.

> **Are you hurting? Pray. Do you feel great? Sing. Are you sick? Call the church leaders together to pray and anoint you with oil in the name of the Master. Believing-prayer will heal you, and Jesus will put you on your feet. And if you've sinned, you'll be forgiven—healed inside and out. Make this your common practice: Confess your sins to each other and pray for each other so that you can live together whole and healed. The prayer of a person living right with God is something powerful to be reckoned with.**
>
> **(James 5:13-17)**

Prayer is not only a personal experience with God but a relational experience with other believers. When God's people come together in united prayer, God hears, provides, delivers, and empowers in answer to their requests. This being true, we must ask ourselves how we can be effective in our church as we come together in corporate prayer.

First, the leaders in our church need prayer. When we come into the worship service, why not be in an attitude of prayer? Pray for the anointing of the Spirit upon the one delivering the message. Pray for those leading the worship. Pray for the choice of music and any individuals ministering to us in music. Why not look around and ask God to show you individuals who may need encouragement, healing, deliverance, or answers to special problems. Most of all, pray for yourself. Confess your sins. Ask God to fill your mind, emotions, and spirit with His Holy Spirit. If each Christian would be in an attitude of prayer, it would transform our worship services.

Receiving the Sacraments

The word *sacrament* is used for something sacred. A sacrament historically became defined as a *visible sign* by which God offers His promises in an outward form. The sacraments are visible elements such as water for baptizing, and bread and wine for the symbol of Jesus' flesh and blood when taking the Lord's Supper. The sacraments are symbols Christ has given us to convey the promises of God. Salvation is **not** through the sacraments. Salvation is **by faith in Christ**. But Christ directly instituted these two sacraments or ordinances for His church to follow: Baptism and the Lord's Supper.

Baptism was instituted by Christ and is to be administered in the name of the Father, Son, and Holy Spirit. It is every Christian's duty to be baptized. It is a sacrament commanded by our Lord. Baptism signifies a washing with water—either by immersion, dipping, or sprinkling.

Does baptism in water wash away sins? Is baptism necessary for salvation? It is only the sacrifice of the blood of Jesus that can wash away sin.

Because of the sacrifice of the Messiah, his blood poured out on the altar of the Cross, we're a free people.

(Ephesians 1:7)

Baptism is a memorial portraying salvation. Water baptism is the new Christian's first act of obedience to Jesus. Baptism is God's object lesson to the world. It illustrates the Gospel story—the cross and resurrection (Christ died for our sins and was raised from the dead on the third day according to the Scripture.) The issue in baptism is not one of salvation, but obedience. What a thrill it is to be buried symbolically and raised again with the Lord Jesus in water baptism. Baptism is a picture of our death to "self" and our resurrection in newness of life. Some churches baptize infants. At the time of confirmation they should be encouraged to personally put their faith in Jesus Christ.

The second ordinance Christ commands us to follow is the **Lord's Supper**. Other terms used for the Lord's Supper are "Communion" and the "Eucharist." The word "Eucharist" means "thanksgiving." This is a practice usually celebrated during worship service. Believers partake of bread and wine (or grape juice) with the purpose of remembering Christ's death on the cross. It is a time for receiving strength from Him and rededicating ourselves to His cause. The bread and the wine are symbols of Christ's broken body and the shedding of His blood. There is the spiritual presence of Christ in the Lord's Supper through the Holy Spirit.

> **Let me go over with you again exactly what goes on in the Lord's Supper and why it is so centrally important. I received my instructions from the Master himself and passed them on to you. The Master, Jesus, on the night of his betrayal, took bread. Having given thanks, he broke it and said,**
>
> **This is my body, broken for you. Do this to remember me. After supper, he did the same thing with the cup:**
>
> **This cup is my blood, my new covenant with you. Each time you drink this cup, remember me. What you must solemnly realize is that every time you eat this bread and every time you drink this cup, you reenact in your words and actions the death of the Master. You will be drawn back to this meal again and again until the Master returns. You must never let familiarity breed contempt.**
>
> **(I Corinthians 11:23-26)**

Fellowship

The need for healthy relationships with other believers in the church is essential for a well-balanced Christian life. Jesus states the identifying mark which Christians are to have:

> **This is how everyone will recognize that you are my disciples—when they see the love you have for each other.**
>
> **(John 13:35)**

We do not function well when we are left to ourselves. God has designed fellowship in the church to be deeply relational. Every Christian has something to contribute to other members of the local church. For the Body of Christ to function effectively, we are all needed. We are all to receive and give love in the family of God. Healing will occur to the degree we are "kindly affectionate to one another with brotherly love."

Stewardship

You can tell a lot about where our hearts are by what we do with our money. Jesus Christ says:

> **"Don't hoard treasure down here where it gets eaten by moths and corroded by rust or—worse!—stolen by burglars. Stockpile treasure in heaven, where it's safe from moth and rust and burglars. It's obvious, isn't it? The place where your treasure is, is the place you will most want to be, and end up being."**

> **(Matthew 6:19-21)**

You cannot read the Book of Acts and understand how Christianity began to spread without noticing that the Christians were generous people, sharing their possessions in proportion to the way God blessed them. Gene Getz in his book entitled *The Walk* points out several directives given by Paul for Christians to follow in their generosity:

1. We should set aside a certain percentage of our income in order to be able to systematically give to God's work.
2. We should be a model to others.
3. We should be accountable.
4. We should be responsive immediately.
5. We should be "faith promise" givers.
6. We should be joyful, willing givers.
7. We should be generous.
8. We should be trusting givers.[21]

> **Remember: A stingy planter gets a stingy crop; a lavish planter gets a lavish crop. I want each of you to take plenty of**

time to think it over, and make up your own mind what you will give. That will protect you against sob stories and arm twisting. God loves it when the giver delights in the giving.

(2 Corinthians 9:6-7)

When we are faithful in our giving, God is faithful to meet our needs. Giving to the church is one method God uses to change our lives from self-centeredness to a life of giving.

Service

In Chapter Eight we learned that the work of the Holy Spirit upon man is for witness and service. Spiritual Gifts are given to those who are Christ's disciples. Everyone receives what God determines is necessary for each one to fulfill the ministry that God has called him to accomplish.

Let's go back and review the section entitled "Paul lists these Spiritual Gifts." Take time to go over all three lists and put a check beside each Spiritual Gift you think you may have. As you participate in the local church, it will soon become evident to you and to others what your Spiritual Gifts are. And as you begin to exercise these Gifts, you will become an effective servant in the church.

Bible Study or Small Groups

Christianity began as people heard the Good News. The message of the Gospel is for all who repent and by faith believe in Jesus Christ and receive the Gift of Eternal Life. Upon that initial contact those new believers were formed into small groups by Jesus' disciples. It was in these small groups that these new Christians were taught "The Apostles' Doctrines." These doctrines were the teachings the Apostles had learned from Jesus Himself.

After Jesus was crucified and resurrected, the Holy Spirit came upon His disciples enabling them to write further instructions to the newly established churches. These "biographies" written about Jesus and the letters or "epistles" sent to these churches, once collected together, became known as the Holy Scriptures or The Bible.

Studying the Bible in small groups is the way the early church began to grow and it is still the most effective means for church growth today. Jesus met with the eleven apostles on a mountain in Galilee and commissioned them to "Go" and "make disciples" of all nations. This was a command and often referred to as the Great Commission.

We have seen some of the benefits in church membership: corporate worship, corporate prayer, receiving the sacraments of the Lord's Supper and baptism, hearing and studying the Word of God, and the opportunity to give to the Lord and others in need. We still need to consider one other benefit.

Training for Disciple-making

He handed out gifts of apostle, prophet, evangelist, and pastor-teacher to train Christ's followers in skilled servant work, working within Christ's body, the church, until we're all moving rhythmically and easily with each other, efficient and graceful in response to God's Son, fully mature adults, fully developed within and without, fully alive like Christ.

(Ephesians 4:11-13)

Jesus' desire is for every Christian to become a disciple-maker. A disciple-maker must be made. This is accomplished by being discipled by a disciple-maker. There are two areas of service in which each church member should be trained. The first is for numerical kingdom growth. The kingdom of God only grows as people receive Jesus Christ as their Savior and Lord. The local church should provide training in how to share the Gospel within the context of each member's sphere of life. As each member shares the Gospel with his family, friends, neighbors, and social contacts, the local church expands.

The second area of service is training its members to minister to those within the Church who have never been discipled, so that they will become disciple-makers. Every member a disciple-maker! So each member has at least a two-fold ministry: ministering to the non-Christian and ministering to his fellow church members. The command in the Great Commission is to *go, baptize, and teach.* These are the elements in making disciples. Disciple-making is the responsibility of the believer, individually. The responsibility to make disciples is given to each and every believer without exception. The local church must provide training so that every member becomes a disciple-maker.

Whenever the old self dominates the Christian, disciple-making will not be practiced. Disciple-making requires obedience to the Great Commission. The success of the early church is attributable to the fact that every Spirit-filled Christian became a disciple-maker.

> **Jesus, undeterred, went right ahead and gave his charge: "God authorized and commanded me to commission you: Go out and train everyone you meet, far and near, in this way of life, marking them by baptism in the threefold name: Father, Son, and Holy Spirit. Then instruct them in the practice of all I have commanded you. I'll be with you as you do this, day after day after day, right up to the end of the age.**
>
> **(Matthew 28:18-20)**

"Internally focused churches concentrate on getting people into the church and generating activity there. These churches may create powerful worship services, excel in teaching, offer thriving youth programs and have vital small groups, but at the end of the day what is measured is the number of people and activities within the church. These are good churches filled with good people. What they do is vital but not sufficient for a healthy church. Worship, teaching, and personal devotions are absolutely necessary for building the internal capacity necessary to sustain an external focus, but if all the human and financial resources are expended inside the four walls of the church, then no matter how "spiritual" things may appear to be, something is missing."[22]

Churches are to be internally strong, but the church must be externally focused. A church which trains its members to fulfill the Great Commission builds bridges into their community instead of walls around their church. An externally focused church sees everyone outside the church as a potential ministry focus.

APPLICATION

1. The church is catholic which means _____.
2. Each member in the family of God has been _____ by God to contribute to the work of the whole body.
3. We have not _____ the Lord until God's Spirit touches our spirit.
4. The New Testament does not prescribe a particular _____ for worship.
5. When the Body of Christ comes into public worship we should come with _____ expecting to hear from God.
6. Christians are to be involved in each other's lives by _____ for each other.
7. Prayer is not only a personal experience with God, but a _____ experience with other Christians.
8. Christ directly instituted two ordinances for his church to follow:

   a) _____

   b) _____

9. It is only the sacrifice of the _____ of Jesus that can wash away sin.
10. _____ is a memorial portraying salvation.
11. The bread and wine used in the Lord's Supper are _____ of Christ's broken body and the shedding of His blood.
12. We should set aside a certain _____ of our income in order to be able to systematically give to God's work.
13. Jesus desire is for _____ Christian to become a disciple-maker.

Assignment

If you have not been baptized, make an appointment with your pastor.

If you have any questions about the Lord's Supper, discuss them with your disciple-maker.

Begin systematically giving to the local church.

CHAPTER TWELVE

MY GOAL: Becoming a Disciple-Maker

How do we fulfill the purpose for our life and reach God's goal? In running any race there must be a goal to reach. We all have goals, but once our goal is reached we settle down to complacency unless we make God's goal our goal.

God's Goal

Through the apostle Paul, God shared His goal for His Son, Jesus. God's goal was that He should have a "Body" through which to express Himself. This Body is called the Church. It is God's desire to express Himself in and through each of His disciples who make up the Church. The goal of our Heavenly Father is to have a vast glorious family for Himself. The Father planted His only unique Son and waits for the growth and harvest of many sons who will one day come to glory.

> **It's in Christ that we find out who we are and what we are living for. Long before we first heard of Christ and got our hopes up, he had his eye on us, had designs on us for glorious living, part of the overall purpose he is working out in everything and everyone.**
>
> **(Ephesians 1:11-12)**

Your goal in fulfilling the Great Commission is by becoming a disciple-maker.

The Magic of Vision

Vision is a picture of what could be, what should be, and what is hoped for. Vision tells us which way to go to get to our goal. If we have not accepted the Great Commission as the marching orders for the church, we will not know Christ's vision for His church. When the vision is communicated, there will be some who stand opposed and refuse to participate, but stay faithful to the dream! This manual has been written to help establish an action plan for helping individuals and churches to fulfill their part in the Great Commission.

Vision tells people what you are asking them to do and why. Vision helps us to think strategically.

The Strategy

God has chosen people, not plans or programs, to spread His message. Personal evangelism is the first step in the process of making disciples. Jesus went out and prayed before He selected a few individuals to follow Him. Before you select someone to disciple, spend time in prayer, making sure the two of you are a fit. You will not be able to disciple just anyone. Men should disciple men, and women disciple women. It stands to reason that since you will be spending considerable time with the person, it is best to disciple the same sex. Jesus knew that a few persons willing to follow Him would become many, if they were properly trained. The disciple-maker must be sensitive to the Holy Spirit in communicating the Good News to unbelievers. The development of a personal relationship demands intimacy. Making disciples requires that the discipler maintain a close personal relationship with those he intends to disciple until they themselves become disciple-makers.

Making disciples cannot be done in a large group. The strategy is that a person is reached with the gospel; then trained in the basic tenets of the Christian faith; is taught how to share his faith with others; and models how to become an effective disciple-maker.

> **And when the Holy Spirit comes on you, you will be able to be my witnesses in Jerusalem, all over Judea and Samaria, even to the ends of the world.**
>
> **(Acts 1:8)**

A careful reading of the Book of Acts reveals that the early Christians were obedient to the Great Commission and became disciple-makers. They had a ministry to the non-Christians (evangelism) and to the Christians who had never been discipled (training.)

> **I'm not saying that I have this all together, that I have it made. But I am well on my way, reaching out for Christ, who has so wondrously reached out for me. Friends, don't get me wrong: By no means do I count myself an expert in all of this, but I've got my eye on the goal, where God is beckoning us onward—to Jesus. I'm off and running, and I'm not turning back.**
>
> **(Philippians 3:12-14)**

Disciple-making can begin with one. In a local church it should begin with the senior pastor, who should lead the journey. Without vision the people perish. All other staff and those in leadership, and finally the membership. in any church should help create the picture: the picture of making disciples. The GOAL is for everyone to become a disciple-making member. Every activity and every person must help in creating the picture.

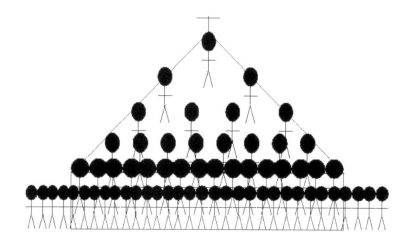

Each member is called upon to share the Good News or the Gospel with those who fall within the context of his/her life.

God has given us the task of telling everyone what he is doing. We're Christ's representatives.

(2 Corinthians 5:18)

1. The gospel has five elements that must be shared. You understand them because you have completed Lesson One. Let's go over them again: God, the creator of the universe, loves all people.
2. God wants us to repent of our sin.
3. God sent His Son Jesus Christ to die on the cross for our sins, and
4. Jesus Christ rose from the dead to purchase for us a place in heaven.
5. We receive Jesus Christ as our Savior and Lord by grace through faith.

We cross over the bridge from our side to His side through prayer. Once you lead someone to Christ, it is your responsibility to disciple that person immediately or find someone who will. If someone has been appointed in your local church as director of discipleship, he/she will help you find a disciple-maker. You will discover as you begin discipling a person that a wonderful friendship will develop. As you go through this **Disciple-making Manual** with your disciple, you will learn to pray with each other, read and discuss the Scriptures together, and have many wonderful discussions about each other's lives. You will be friends for life! You will become the example God wants you to become by modeling how to disciple someone else.

Remember, the goal is not to disciple someone, but to reproduce Christ's life in your disciple by training him/her to become a disciple-maker. Disciple-making is a way of life. It is not something you do yourself; it is something the Holy Spirit does through you.

Reward! Recognize! Retain!

Make sure new disciple-makers are recognized immediately, genuinely, and in public. This will motivate others to follow in their steps. Accountability to another person is crucial in running any race. A disciple must be made by a disciple-maker. Accountability to a disciple-maker is essential to becoming a disciple-maker yourself. We all need other people to help us keep our commitments. God calls ordinary people with a focused task of disciple-making. Commitment involves obedience to the command of Jesus in the Great Commission to "Make Disciples." The central vision for every Christian is The Great Commission.

Disciple-making is not as much a strategy as it is a transformation. It moves people into the lives of others by loving and serving. It is a life of giving. Jesus' command to His disciples was to "make disciples of all the nations." Therefore, the strategy would have to be applicable to all cultures, under any political system, and to all social settings. There is no segment of society in which disciple-making cannot be applied. Making disciples never becomes obsolete. It should never be replaced by something else. It is the life-line of the church.

The only Good Idea is the one that Works

Does disciple-making really work?

Philippine Student Alliance Lay Movement

The Philippine Student Alliance Lay Movement (PSALM), in a matter of six years, grew from three members to over ten thousand. The founder of

PSALM, Dr. Joseph Arthur, was appointed by the Christian and Missionary Alliance (CMA) Church as a missionary to the Philippines. He had a vision to reach the college and university population with the Gospel, and to disciple the new believers until they became disciple-makers.

It would be difficult to find a country that would be more diverse. In the Philippines with its 7,000 islands, the people speak thirteen different languages. Their cultural and religious backgrounds are diverse. Roman Catholicism is the predominate religion, followed by Islam, and Protestantism. The social structure is volcanic, consisting of five percent of the population owning ninety-five percent of the wealth. Politically, the government is a shaky democratic republic. The second largest island in the south, Mindanao, has the largest Muslim population. It has a goal of separation from the present government to form its own Islamic state. The Philippines has long struggled with a Marxist/ Maoist influence throughout its borders. In 1974 the former president, Ferdinand Marcos, declared Marshal Law to try to stem the tide of communism.

The Philippines has the second largest college and university student population in the world next to the United States per capita population. The more than one million students attend one of the seven hundred colleges and universities each year.

In the midst of all this diversity PSALM, with its multiplication of disciples working on sixty-five campuses throughout the Philippines, is a bright and shining example of disciple-making working in a diverse nation.

Friendship Bible Church of Keystone Heights, Florida

Does disciple-making work in an area with limited population? Keystone Heights, Florida, has a population of around two thousand. There is one stoplight in the center of the town. Eight churches exist to serve this population. One of those churches is The Friendship Bible Church. The pastor, along with the church governing body and membership, decided to provide each household in the community the opportunity to hear the gospel and receive Jesus Christ as their Savior and Lord. In a systematic way the church members made contact with others in the community. Those who decided to become followers of Jesus were discipled and became members of the local church. Today this church with its four hundred members is a testimony that disciple-making works.

Santa Rosa Alliance Church, Santa Rosa, California

From Florida to California disciple-making works. One of the oldest Christian and Missionary Alliance Churches exists in Santa Rosa, California. Santa Rosa, the city of roses, with a population of nearly 200,000, is forty miles north of San Francisco. Situated on the Russian River and on the outskirts of Santa Rosa is the town of Guerneville, known as a center for lesbian and homosexual activity. In 1990 the Russian River overflowed and the town was under water. Many of the residents were airlifted to safety. Others were trapped by washed out bridges. Food, clothing, and other essentials became very scarce. The members of the Santa Rosa Alliance Church collected truckloads of food, water, clothing, and personal items to distribute to those in need in that community. Social concern is part of discipleship with no strings attached.

Life-changing discipleship was the strategy of this church. The senior pastor was the motivator, leader, and first disciple-maker to this congregation. Then his staff, church governing board, elders, deacons, deaconesses, and members followed. Knowing that evangelism is the first step in disciple-making, the Minister of Evangelism was sent to Coral Ridge Presbyterian Church in Fort Lauderdale, Florida, for training in "Evangelism Explosion." The Santa Rosa Alliance Church became a training base for "Evangelism Explosion" on the west coast.

Disciple-making in The Santa Rosa Alliance Church took on the two-way approach to disciple-making: to the non-Christians and to the members of the church. As individuals received Christ as their Savior and Lord, they were immediately assigned a disciple-maker. Those within the church were enrolled in the life-changing discipleship training with the goal of every member becoming a disciple-maker. Disciple-making is God's method for kingdom building. It is for every church!

The First United Methodist Church of DeLand, Florida

Rev. Owen Stricklin is the senior minister at The First United Methodist Church of DeLand, Florida. His wife, Barbara, is the director of discipleship. The church is located in the downtown section of the city and has been in the same location for over 100 years. Both Owen and Barbara caught the vision of disciple-making as God's method of reaching the community and the world.

In an interview I asked Owen what he thought was the DNA of this church. His response was "every member being obedient to the Great Commission by making disciples." Barbara insisted that the pastor and staff must model disciple-making as a way of life. With this as their emphasis, in the past two years they have trained nearly one hundred disciple-makers in their church.

The fire of disciple-making is a flame that cannot go out. FUMC understands that the culture in which the members of the church live must meet the needs of the people in their life context. In analyzing their community one discovery they made was the number of homeless people who roam the streets and sleep in parks and wooded areas around the city. They soon opened an area of their church to feed the hungry, clothe the needy, encourage the depressed and down-trodden, and find employment for those capable of working. The testimonies that could be shared about transformed lives are too numerous to mention.

Another area of concern was the youth of the city. Funds were set aside for the development of a youth center that provides fellowship, musical involvement, recreation, computer training, spiritual encounter and guidance. Disciple-making is the key to successful youth work.

A First Response Team was organized for assisting families at a time of crisis. In 2006, when several families were in harm's way of three terrible hurricanes, this team of trained experts was on the scene ministering in love in whatever way they could.

Owen and Barbara Stricklin do not have tunnel vision seeing only their own community, but they have a vision for the world. Mission Teams are organized and sent out every year to other countries to help in whatever way they can, but they never lose sight of the disciple-making ministry that God has called all of us to fulfill.

> **Use your heads as you live and work among outsiders. Don't miss a trick. Make the most of every opportunity. Be gracious in your speech. The goal is to bring out the best in others in a conversation, not put them down, not cut them out.**
>
> **(Colossians 4:5-6)**

All disciples who have gone before us tell us to strip down, start running, and don't quit. An Olympian is trained the same way. Strip down, start running, and don't quit. We may fall, we may stumble; but if we do, get up, keep running and win.

Hebrews 12:1-2 gives us the rules for running the race.

> **Do you see what this means—all these pioneers who blazed the way, all these veterans cheering us on? It means we'd better get on with it. Strip down, start running—and never quit! No extra spiritual fat, no parasitic sins. Keep your eyes on *Jesus*, who both began and finished this race we're in. Study how he did it. Because he never lost sight of where he was headed—that exhilarating finish in and with God—he could put up with anything along the way: Cross, shame, whatever. And now he's there, in the place of honor, right alongside God. When you find yourself flagging in your faith, go over that story again, item by item, that long litany of hostility he plowed through. *That* will shoot adrenaline into your souls!**

(Hebrews:12:1-2)

Here are the rules:

1. No extra spiritual fat
2. No parasitic sins
3. Keep your eyes on Jesus

What a glorious day that will be when we stand before God and meet the people in heaven with whom we have had the privilege to share the Gospel and discipled them until they, in turn, became disciple-makers. You will hear your Heavenly Father say, "Well done, good and faithful servant" because God keeps the scoreboard.

As we come to the close of these training sessions, I want to ask you several important questions.

1. Are you willing to verbally share the good news that brings eternal life?
2. Are you willing to become a disciple-maker as a way of life?
3. Are you willing to serve all humanity in a spirit of compassion and love?

God's command to all believers is: **GO, MAKE DISCIPLES!**

DO IT BECAUSE IT IS THE RIGHT THING TO DO

LET'S GET STARTED !!

Steps in beginning a disciple-making strategy in a local church

1. Your minister should take the lead and set the vision for the church of everyone becoming a disciple-maker.
2. Your minister should disciple the first disciple and appoint them as the director of disciple-making.
3. The director of disciple-making should begin praying for the next person to disciple.
4. See everyone within and outside the church as a potential disciple-maker.
5. Disciple one person at a time until they become a disciple-maker.
6. Explain the requirements to every potential disciple-maker for becoming a disciple-maker.

(Requirements)

a) They must agree to meet with their discipler a total of twelve times. The frequency and place of meetings will be determined by you and your discipler.

b) Each session will be sixty minutes. You will supply a copy of the book *The Twelve Essentials for Disciple-Making by Dr. Joseph Arthur,* (You may use any other material for disciple-making that you choose.

c) All requirements in each lesson must be completed before you begin the next session.

d) You are required to be on time when an appointment is scheduled with your discipler.

e) You will be encouraged at the first session to begin praying for a possible person that you can begin discipling. Once you have completed a lesson you may teach that same lesson to a disciple of your own.

7. In the first session go over the requirements, have prayer for your disciple, and inform them that you are going to demonstrate how each lesson is to be taught.
8. Begin by taking turns reading one paragraph at a time. First is the discipler, and then the disciple. Answer any questions that may arise.

YOU HAVE JUST BEGUN THE MOST EXCITING MINISTRY YOU COULD EVER HAVE!

GOD BLESS!

APPLICATION

1. All disciples that have gone before us tell us to strip down, start running and don't _____.

2. The Scriptures list the rules for running the race.

   a) No extra spiritual fat.
   b) No parasitic sins.
   c) _____.

3. _____ involves obedience to the command of Jesus in the Great Commission.

4. _____ is a picture of what could be and what you hope for.

5. It is God's desire to express Himself in and through each of his _____.

6. God has chosen _____ not plans or programs of to Spread His message.

7. Personal _____ is the first step in the process of making disciples.

8. _____ is a way of life.

9. There is no segment of society in which _____ cannot be applied.

10. _____ concern is all part of discipleship with no strings being attached.

Assignment

You should discuss with your disciple-maker how to go about setting up An appointment with a family member, a friend, or a neighbor. Your disciple-maker may set up an appointment for you. "He/she will demonstrate, in a live setting, how to share the Gospel with someone else."

ANSWERS TO REVIEW EXERCISES

Chapter One

Application

1. God **loves** all the human race.
2. What destroys our relationship with God?
   Selfishness or Sin.
3. The message of the Bible is for **all** the human race.
4. When we confess our sin and turn from it and go in the opposite direction, this process is called **repentance.**
5. We need **forgiveness** because we are all sinful.
6. God wants to have a **relationship** with us.
7. **Saving Faith** is trusting Jesus Christ alone for our salvation.
8. God offers us a **gift** of grace.
9. The bridge from our side to His side is called **the cross.**
10. What does it mean to "cross over"?

    a) *To receive Jesus Christ as Savior*
    b) *To receive God's promise of a place in heaven.*

11. How do I know I have received the gift of Eternal Life?

    a) *The Bible tells me so.*
    b) *A confirmation of the Holy Spirit with my spirit.*

12. Name two things that will happen in your life when you become a Christian.
    Love for others.
    A hunger for the Word of God.
    A greater aware of right and wrong.
    A desire to share with others what God has done in your life.
    A desire to follow the Lord in baptism.

Chapter Two

Application

1. Why did God create man?
   To bring glory to God.
2. God made only one creature, *man,* to be made in "the image of God."
3. What was the first thing God created in relation to man?
   His physical body.
4. Our *physical bodies* are the means by which we communicate with others.
5. The word *"soul"* means "being" or "person."
6. Our *mind, will, and emotions* are functions of the "soul."
7. God created our *spirit* to allow us access to God's Person.
8. Redemption is necessary because sin distorted the *image of God* in man and corrupted man's *nature.*
9. The goal of *redemption* is to conform us to the image of Jesus Christ.
10. *Adoption* is an act of God whereby He makes us members of His family.
11. *Glorification* for man takes place when we receive our resurrected bodies.
12. List the four stages of God's Plan for us:
    Created Sons of God
    Redeemed Sons of God
    Adopted Sons of God
    Glorified Sons of God

Chapter Three

Application

1. A ***disciple*** is a student, learner, or a pupil.
2. What is the disciple's business?

   a. ***Being a witness***
   b. ***Becoming a disciple-maker***

3. What are the four keys to becoming a disciple-maker?

   a. ***Dependence on the Holy Spirit***
   b. ***"Go" and explain the gospel to unbelievers.***
   c. ***Encourage new believers to be baptized.***
   d. ***Instruct believers in the basic principle of the Christian faith.***

4. The Great Commission is not an ***option*** but a ***command.***
5. After 70 A.D. the early church was called ***catholic,*** meaning universal.
6. The crisis in the Church after the second century was:
   (Circle the correct answer)

   a. The laity lost its vision for ministry.
   b. The clergy took over the ministry.
   c. The Great Commission was disobeyed by many.
   d. ***All the above***

7. Where does a disciple go to make contacts?
   Your sphere of ***influence***
8. You are a ***minister*** of God

Chapter Four

Application

1. The Bible consists of how many Books?
   Sixty-Six
2. Name the two parts of the Bible.
   The Old and New Testaments
3. The *Old Testament* reveals the sinfulness of mankind and looks forward to the coming of Jesus.
4. The *New Testament* tells of the entrance of God into the world in the person of Jesus Christ.
5. The word "inspiration" means *God-breathed.*
6. The *Bible* is the Word of God.
7. Who should read the Bible?
   Everyone
8. The most effective character-forming power we know is:
   Bible Reading.
9. The purpose of studying the Bible is the total _____ of the person.
10. What are the four basic steps in studying the Bible?

Humility
Understanding
Interpretation
Application

Chapter Five

Application

1. Prayer is a **two-way** communication with God. It is our expression of our desire to do the Will of God, and God's expression to us communicating what His Will is for us.
2. The acrostic ACTS is an aid to prayer. Each letter indicates a vital element of prayer.
   Adoration—reverence and praise.
   Confession—coming to God and saying, "I need help."
   Thanksgiving—A spirit of appreciation for God's mercy and grace.
   Supplication—prayer for others and prayer for ourselves.
3. Jesus taught His disciples to pray with **simplicity;** addressed to **God;** and to pray in **the name of Jesus** .
4. How do we draw near to God?

   a. Spend **time** in prayer.
   b. Pray **specifically.**
   c. Pray according to the **Will of God.**
   d. Pray in the **Spirit.**

5. What are the three ways God answers prayer?

   a. **Yes**
   b. **No**
   c. **Wait**

Chapter Six

Application

Answer the following questions.

1. Who is the Holy Spirit?
   The Holy Spirit is **God** and He is a person.
2. All who believe in Jesus Christ as their Savior and Lord have **The Holy Spirit** in them.
3. The Holy Spirit **clothes** us with Christ by helping us understand God's Word and joins with our spirit restoring our relationship with God; grants us God's mark of ownership; places us into the Body of Christ; and controls us to do the Will of God.
4. The Bible refers to someone who has never received Christ as Savior as an **unspiritual self.**
5. When you become a Christian, the Bible refers to you as **spiritually alive.**
6. When Christians become selfish, the Bible refers to them as **infants.**
7. **Spiritual Breathing** means exhaling or confessing our sins, and inhaling God's forgiveness.
8. Cleansing from sin, allowing the Holy Spirit to be Lord of our mind, submitting our emotions to the Holy Spirit, obeying God's Will; and yielding our whole personality to The Holy Spirit are steps in how to be **controlled** by the Holy Spirit.
9. List two good things that result from being controlled by the Holy Spirit.
   Effective service and **Holy living**

Chapter Seven

Application

1. ***Humility*** can only be accomplished by brokenness.
2. ***Brokenness*** means that we in humility are willing to offer ourselves completely to God.
3. A ***clear conscience*** is knowing that no one, God or man, can point a finger at you and say, "You've offended me and you've never asked for my forgiveness."
4. In asking for forgiveness you must reflect sincere ***repentance.***
5. ***Meekness*** is a sign of humility.
6. Meekness is something that is produced by the ***Holy Spirit.***
7. Three sources of irritations are:

    a) ***Personal handicaps***
    b) ***Environment***
    c) ***People***

8. God allows irritations to come into our lives to develop ***character qualities.***
9. ***Joy*** is the mark of maturity.

Chapter Eight

Application

1. It is not a person's position that makes him great, but the **attitude of serving anyone in need.**
2. It will cost a Christian disciple nothing less than his **life** to find fulfillment as God's servant.
3. The fruit of the Spirit consists of **character** qualities describing the life of Christ.
4. **Legalism** is the belief that one can earn one's way by service to God and to others.
5. True service is based on **love** and gratitude.
6. **Blinds** are methods we use that reveal the selfish life.
7. God wants us to have open **windows** so the character of Christ is seen.
8. Every quality in the list of the Fruit of the Spirit is a facet of divine **love.**
9. f a person has the proper life within and the outpouring of the Spirit without, he can be very **useful** to the Lord.
10. A person may possess spiritual **gifts** while being spiritually immature.
11. Every child of God receives spiritual gifts at **God's** discretion.
12. Spiritual gifts are to be exercised for the building up of the **Church.**

Chapter Nine

Application

1. *Everyone* will acknowledge Jesus Christ as Lord, willingly or unwillingly.
2. Acknowledging Jesus as Lord means that I have. *confessed* with my mouth and *believed* in my heart that Jesus Christ is the Gift of Eternal Life.
3. The Bible promises that those who truly seek to please Him will get the *directions* they need from Him.
4. God's divine way of living is produced only by *God's Spirit* and is a life of giving.
5. Our Heavenly Father desires to have His sons *express* His life in and through us.
6. This new life in Christ with God is accomplished by the *cross* .
7. A life of *giving* is God's way and plan.
8. In submission we become free to *value* other people. Jesus, others, and self is the proper order.
9. Our self-denials and Christ's *resurrection* power in us prepare us for the practical outflow for service.
10. The divine way of life results in His resurrection power and *fruitfulness.*

Chapter Ten

Application

1. Difficulties that come from God come in the form of *discipline.*
2. *Chastisement* is an act of God used as God's method for building character.
3. *Reapings* occur when we violate natural law.
4. Satan is the source of *hindrances.*
5. How do good angels help us defeat our enemies?
   They guard and protect us.
6. The term *Satan* means adversary.
7. Evil angelic spirits are called *demons.*
8. List five methods Satan uses to attack the Christian.

   a) *Temptation*
   b) *Deception*
   c) *Illness*
   d) *Accusations*
   c) *Discouragement*

9. List the eight pieces of spiritual armor God has provided for us.
   Truth—Righteousness—Peace—Faith—Salvation—Sword of the Spirit—Prayer—Love
10. *Love* is the greatest of all the gifts

Chapter Eleven

Application

1. The church is "catholic" which means **universal.**
2. Each member in the family of God has been **gifted** by God to contribute to the work of the whole body.
3. We have not **worshiped** the Lord until God's Spirit touches our spirit.
4. The New Testament does not prescribe a particular **form** for worship.
5. When the Body of Christ comes into public worship we should come with **anticipation**, expecting to hear from God.
6. Christians are to be involved in each other's lives by **praying** for each other.
7. Prayer is not only a personal experience with God, but a **relational** experience with other Christians.
8. Christ directly instituted two ordinances for His church to follow:

    a. **Baptism**
    b. **The Lord's Supper**

9. It is only the sacrifice of the **blood** of Jesus that can wash away sin.
10. **Baptism** is a memorial portraying salvation.
11. The bread and wine used in the Lord's Supper are **symbols** of Christ's broken body and the shedding of His blood.
12. We should set aside a certain **percentage** of our income in order to be able to systematically give to God's work.
13. Jesus' desire is for **every** Christian to become a disciple-maker.

Chapter Twelve

Application

1. It is God's desire to express Himself in and through each of his *disciples.*
2. God has chosen *people* not plans or programs to spread his message.
3. Personal *evangelism* is the first step in the process of making disciples.
4. *Vision* is a picture of what could be and what you hope for.
5. *Commitment* involves obedience to the command of Jesus in the Great Commission.
6. *Disciple-making* is a way of life.
7. There is no segment of society in which *disciple-making* cannot be applied.
8. *Social* concern is all part of discipleship with no strings being attached.
9. All disciples who have gone before us tell us to strip down, start running, and don't *quit.*
10. The Scriptures list the rules for running the race.

    a. No extra spiritual fat.
    b. No parasitic sins.
    c. *Keep your eyes on Jesus.*

Summary of Twelve Essentials of Disciple-Making

The Great Commission informs us that we are to disciple everyone who has not been discipled. We can help other Christians to mature by encouraging them to become disciple-makers. This is a fulfilling ministry and is a command given to us by Jesus Himself: **MAKE DISCIPLES!**

> **Our firm decision is to work from this focused center: One man died for everyone. That puts everyone in the same boat. He included everyone in his death so that everyone could also be included in his life, a resurrection life, a far better like than people ever lived on their own.**

> **(2 Corinthians 5:17-20)**

From the beginning the disciples preached the resurrection of Jesus. On the Day of Pentecost the apostle Peter preached telling those in attendance to repent and be baptized in the name of Jesus.

> **Change your life. Turn to God and be baptized, each of you, in the name of Jesus Christ, so your sins are forgiven. Receive the gift of the Holy Spirit.**

> **(Acts 2:38)**

Many accepted Peter's invitation. They were baptized and about three thousand were added to the Jesus movement that day. That is how the Christian church started. It was quite a beginning. The first forty years saw the infant church spread at a phenomenal rate. It sprang up in most major cities in the Roman Empire and was transformed into a fellowship of many different peoples. The disciples called their new movement, "The Way." They meant by it a gathering of God's people.

The Apostle Paul's converts were a mixed lot. He was concerned about instilling Christian principles in those who gathered to worship Jesus Christ. He established churches by discipleship. He called unbelievers to repentance and instructed believers in the teachings of the apostles.

For practical purposes A.D. 70 and the destruction of Jerusalem mark the end of the apostolic period. Most of the original apostles were dead, and the churches they had founded had passed into new hands. In the period that followed, Christianity spread throughout the Roman Empire. Christians realized that they were a part of a rapidly expanding movement. They called it "catholic," suggesting that it was universal.

The early church grew because everyone was ministering to others by being a witness and they were discipling new believers. Following Pentecost everyone was in awe because the believers lived in a wonderful harmony. They understood the need for relationships. Everyone was discipling someone else. Christianity was a spiritual explosion. The disciples had a spiritual vision and a conviction that all believers should be ministers.

> **They followed a daily discipline of worship in the Temple Followed by meals at home, every meal a celebration, Exuberant and joyful, as they praised God. People in General liked what they saw. Every day their numbers grew as God added those who were saved.**
>
> **(Acts 2:46-47)**

Soon a crisis arose. The Christians began to lose their vision and ignored Jesus' command to fulfill The Great Commission. No one seems to know just how the single pastor, assisted by the elders and deacons, became the widespread pattern within the churches, but we know it did. Before long, instead of being empowered by the Holy Spirit, they relied on the clergy to do the work of ministry.

To face the challenges of their times the Christians turned increasingly to their bishops for spiritual leadership. By the late second century the unchallenged leader in church affairs was the bishop. These changes in the structure and functioning of the church created institutionalism that has devastated the Church to this day. In the first and second centuries,

Christians looked for proof of the Spirit's power not in an office, but in the lives of believers. The Apostle Paul described the Spirit's work in terms of the edification of the entire church. This edification means growth in all that is good.

> **But what happens when we live God's way? He brings Gifts into our lives, much the same way that fruit appears In an orchard—things like affection for others, exuberance about life, serenity. We develop a willingness to stick with things, a sense of compassion in the heart, and a conviction that a basic holiness permeates things and people. We find ourselves involved in loyal commitments.**
>
> **(Galatians 5:22-23)**

Effective disciple-making means every believer is to be a witness to unbelievers and disciple them until they are mature enough to disciple others and in turn fulfill the Great Commission. Warren Wiersbe in his *Bible Exposition Commentary,* points out the necessity of disciple-making. "In many respects, we have departed from this pattern. In most churches, the congregation pays the pastor to preach, win the lost, and build up the saved—while the church members function as cheerleaders (if they are enthusiastic) or spectators. The converts' are won, baptized, and given the right hand of fellowship, then they join the other spectators. How much faster our churches would grow, and how much stronger and happier our church members would be, if each one were discipling another believer. The only way a local church can be fruitful and multiply instead of growing by addition is with a systematic discipleship program".

We must get back to disciple-making. It is not an option; it is a command and the responsibility of every believer.

Endnotes

1   Robert Schuller, *Life's Not Fair but God is Good,* (Thomas Nelson Publishers, Nashville, Tennessee, 1991). p.251.

2   Mark Mittelberg, Lee Strobel, Bill Hybels, *Becoming a Contagious Christian,* (Zondervan Publishing House, Grand Rapids, Michigan, 1995.) pp. 65. Adopted from *The Bridge,* 1981 by The Navigators, NavPress, Colorado Springs, Colorado.

3   *Ibid. 66.*

4   Mike Breen, Walt Kallestad, *The Passionate Church,* (Cook Communications, Paris, Ontario, 2005.) p. 39.

5   Wayne Gruden, *Systematic Theology,* (Zondervan Publishing House, Grand Rapids, Michigan, 1994.) p.736.

6   DeVern Fromke, *The Ultimate Intention,* (Sure Foundation, Mt. Vernon, Mo. 1963.) The materials in this chapter is summarized from Chapter 9, pp. 60-64.

7   Jack Hayford, *Answering the Call to Evangelism: Spreading the Good News to Everyone,* (Thomas Nelson Inc., Nashville, Tennessee, 1995) Lesson 1, The Call to Evangelism.

8   Ibid. Lesson 1

9   Bruce L. Shelley, *Church History in Plain Language,* (Word Publishing, Dallas, Texas, 1982). P.85.

10   Warren Wiersbe, *The Bible Exposition Commentary, Vol. 1 (Victor Books,* Scripture Press Publication Inc. Wheaton, Ill., 1989.) pp. 107-108.

11   Steve Collins, *Christian Discipleship,* (Virgil W. Hensley Inc., Tulsa, OK, 1988) p.170.

12   Hayford, Ibid, Lesson 1

13   Herbert Lockyer Sr. (editor), *Nelson's Illustrated Bible Dictionary.* (Thomas Nelson Publisher, Nashville, Tennessee, 1086.) p.508.

14   Peter M. Lord, *ACTS*, (Agape Ministries, Titusville, Florida, 1987.) p.12.

15   Collins, Ibid. p.153

16   William Law, *A Serious Call to a Devout and Holy Life*. (Nashville Upper Room Press, Nashville, Tennessee, 1952.) p.26.

17   Fromke, Ibid. (The material in this chapter is summarized from chapter 15, pp.96-99.)

18   Foster, Ibid., pp.122-123.

19   Gruden, Ibid. p.307.

20   Wiersbe, Ibid., Vol. 2, p.58.

21   Gene Getz, *The Walk*, (Broadman and Holman Publishers, Nashville, Tennessee, 1994.) pp.150-154.

22   Rick Rusaw, Eric Swanson, *The Externally Focused Church,* (Group Publishing Inc., Loveland, Colorado, 2004) p. 16.

Made in the USA
Middletown, DE
06 November 2014